EXCEL 2000

in easy steps

STEPHEN COPESTAKE

COMPUTER STEP

In easy steps is an imprint of Computer Step
Southfield Road . Southam
Warwickshire CV47 OFB . England

http://www.ineasysteps.com

Notice of Liability

Every effort has been made to ensure that this book contains accurate
and current information. However, Computer Step and the author shall
not be liable for any loss or damage suffered by readers as a result of
any information contained herein.

Trademarks

Microsoft® and Windows® are registered trademarks of Microsoft
Corporation. All other trademarks are acknowledged as belonging to
their respective companies.

Printed and bound in the United Kingdom

ISBN 1-84078-035-5

Table Of Contents

Getting started

In this chapter, you'll learn about the Excel 2000 screen, and about basic terminology. You'll also discover how to use/customise toolbars, and enter data. You'll navigate through and between Excel worksheets, and become proficient in selection techniques. You'll also learn how to use Excel 2000's comprehensive HELP system (including the Office Assistant) and Quick File Switching. Finally, you'll have Excel detect basic errors and repair them.

Covers

Chapter One

The Excel 2000 screen

Below is a detailed illustration of the Excel 2000 screen:

Title bar   Menu bar   Column letters

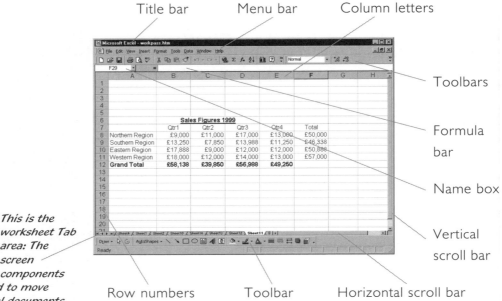

Toolbars

Formula bar

Name box

Vertical scroll bar

This is the worksheet Tab area: The screen components here are used to move through Excel documents.

Row numbers   Toolbar   Horizontal scroll bar

Some of these screen components can be hidden at will.

Specifying which screen components display

Pull down the Tools menu and click Options. Then:

Activate the View tab

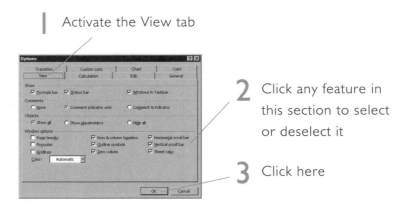

2 Click any feature in this section to select or deselect it

3 Click here

Screen components in detail

Cells occur where rows and columns intersect.

Components shown in the opening screen on page 8 are explained in more detail now:

The worksheet

This is the large central rectangular area which is subdivided into a grid of cells. The cells are used to store data.

The Excel 2000 Control menu looks like this:

The Title Bar

The Title Bar contains the program title and the name of the overall Excel workbook. It also contains (at the left-hand end) the button for the pull-down Control menu.

One way to close Excel 2000 is to double-click this button with the left-hand mouse button.

The Menu Bar

This contains menu titles for all the commands used to build, format and control Excel worksheets. Clicking any title with the left mouse button will display a pull-down menu from which various options may be selected.

For a more detailed definition of worksheets and workbooks, see page 15.

Toolbars

Toolbars are collections of icons representing the most commonly used commands required for standard tasks. By clicking an icon, you initiate the command. This represents a major saving in time and effort.

Excel 2000 comes with some 15 toolbars, of which perhaps the most commonly used are:

Menus and toolbars are also self-customising – see pages 13-14.

- Standard

- Formatting

- Web

See pages 11-12 and 14 for how to customise and work with toolbars.

...cont'd

For how to use the vertical and horizontal scroll bars to navigate through Excel 2000 worksheets, see page 21.

The Formula Bar

This displays the location and contents of the currently selected cell. The Formula Bar represents a particularly useful way to enter:

- formulas

- other cell data (e.g. text)

Column headings

Column headings define each cell within a given column horizontally. Columns are labelled A, B, C, etc.

Row headings

Row headings define each cell within a given row vertically. Rows are numbered 1, 2, 3, etc.

To create your own toolbar, pull down the Tools menu and click Customize. In the Customize dialog, select the Toolbars tab. Click:

New...

In the Toolbar name: field in the New Toolbar dialog, name the new toolbar. Click OK.

(To add buttons to your new toolbar, follow the procedures on page 12.)

The Vertical Scroll Bar

This enables you to move the visible window vertically up and down the worksheet, under the control of the mouse.

The Horizontal Scroll Bar

This enables you to move the visible window horizontally to the left or right across the worksheet.

Sheet tabs

These enable you to select which spreadsheet should be displayed. By clicking on a sheet tab, you jump to the relevant sheet.

(You can also use sheet tabs to perform operations on more than one worksheet at a time.)

The Office Assistant

The Office Assistant is an interactive source of help. See pages 25-28 for how to use it.

Working with toolbars

To strip the screen so it contains only the Menu bar and Row/ Column headings (a technique which makes it easier to work with large worksheets), pull down the View menu and click Full Screen.

To return to the normal view, do the following:

Click here

Toolbars are important components in Excel 2000. A toolbar is an on-screen bar which contains shortcut buttons. These symbolise and allow easy access to often-used commands which would normally have to be invoked via one or more menus.

For example, Excel 2000's Standard toolbar lets you:

- create, open, save and print documents

- perform copy & paste and cut & paste operations

- undo editing actions

- access Excel's HELP system

by simply clicking on the relevant button.

You can control which toolbars display.

Specifying which toolbars are visible

Pull down the View menu and click Toolbars. Now do the following:

Toolbars are self-customising – see page 14 for more information.

Carrying out step 1 in respect of a toolbar which already has a ✔ against it hides it instead.

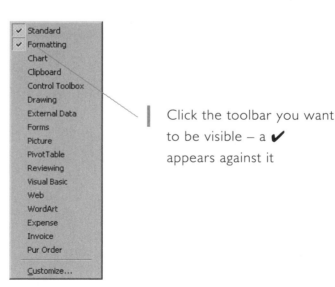

Click the toolbar you want to be visible – a ✔ appears against it

Repeat this procedure for as many toolbars as necessary.

...cont'd

To remove a toolbar button, launch the Customize dialog. Then drag the button off the toolbar onto the worksheet. Release the mouse button. Finally, perform step 5.

See page 14 for another way to add/remove buttons in toolbars.

Repeat steps 2 to 4 as often as necessary.

To find out what a button does, click the Description button after step 3. Excel launches a help bubble:

Save (File menu)
Saves the active file with its current file name, location, and file format.

Press Esc to clear it.

Adding buttons to toolbars

By default, the pre-defined toolbars which come with Excel 2000 have only a relatively small number of buttons associated with them. However, just about all editing operations you can perform from within Excel menus can be incorporated as a button within the toolbar of your choice, for convenience and ease of access.

To do this, first make sure the toolbar you want to add one or more buttons to is visible (see page 11 for how to do this). Move the mouse pointer over the toolbar and right-click once. In the menu which appears, click Customize. Now do the following:

1 Ensure this tab is active

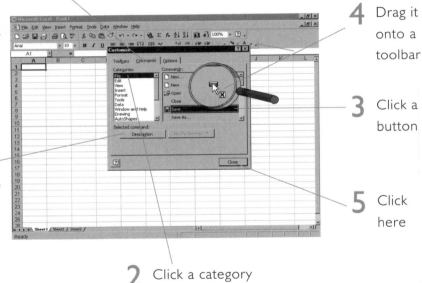

4 Drag it onto a toolbar

3 Click a button

5 Click here

2 Click a category

Automatic customisation

A long-standing anomaly in the use of software has been that, although different users use different features, no allowance has been made for this: the same program features display on everyone's menus and toolbars...

Now this has changed. In Excel 2000, menus and toolbars are personalised.

Personalised menus

Excel 2000 menus expand automatically. Simply pull down the required menu, (which will at first be abbreviated) then wait a few seconds: it expands to display the full menu.

However, to expand them manually, click here on the chevrons at the bottom of the menu:

When you first use Excel 2000, its menus display the features which Microsoft believes are used 95% of the time. Features which are infrequently used are not immediately visible. This is made clear in the illustrations below:

Excel 2000's View menu, as it first appears...

As you use Excel 2000, individual features are dynamically promoted or demoted in the relevant menus.

The fact that menus are continually evolving means that your menus may differ slightly from illustrations in this book.

The expanded menu – the (currently) little-used features are shown in paler grey

As you use Excel 2000, individual features are dynamically promoted or demoted in the relevant toolbars.

As a result, your toolbars may differ slightly from illustrations in this book.

Personalised toolbars

Toolbars in Excel 2000 work on a similar principle to menus:

- if possible, they display on a single row

- they overlap when there isn't enough room on-screen

- icons are 'promoted' and 'demoted' like menu entries

Look at the illustration below:

Click here

You can use this fly-out as an alternative way to add/ remove buttons in toolbars.

Place the mouse pointer over Add or Remove Buttons. In the menu which appears, do one of the following:

- *click an entry which doesn't have* ✓ *against it to add it to the toolbar*

- *click an entry which does have* ✓ *against it to remove it from the toolbar*

Here, two of Excel 2000's toolbars (Standard & Formatting) are displaying side by side. As a result, not all of the buttons display. Following step 1 above produces this result:

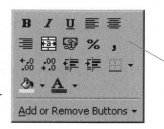

Icons Excel has determined are (currently) little used display in a separate fly-out

To implement any of the hidden features, simply click the relevant icon.

Basic terminology

Here, we explore some of the basic terms used throughout Excel 2000.

Worksheets

'Worksheet' is Excel's name for a spreadsheet. Worksheets are arrays of cells used to store data. This often involves simple arithmetical calculations linking the cells together in tables, usually for some kind of analysis.

Worksheets are the essential building-blocks of workbooks – see below.

By default, Excel workbooks contain 3 worksheets:

- *Sheet 1*
- *Sheet 2*
- *Sheet 3*

Workbooks

A workbook is a file which holds together a collection of worksheets (and possibly charts – for more information on charts, see Chapter 14). It will be seen in later chapters that it is usual to have several worksheets linked together and often convenient to summarise the data on these worksheets in the form of associated charts or graphs.

See Chapter 4 for more information on workbooks.

When you create a new document in Excel, you're actually creating a new workbook. Each new workbook has a default name: Book 1, Book 2 etc.

The Worksheet Window

The opening Excel 2000 window displays (typically):

- 9 columns labelled A to L

- 18 rows labelled 1 to 25

The exact number of rows and columns shown depends on the screen size, video driver and resolution.

It must be appreciated that this is only the extreme top left-hand corner of the full worksheet which extends to:

This means each worksheet contains 16,777,216 cells.

- 256 columns labelled A to Z then AA to IV

- 65,536 rows labelled 1 to 65,536

See the illustration on page 16 for further clarification.

As we've just seen, the Excel 2000 screen displays only a tiny section of the available worksheet. The illustration below displays this graphically:

This area covers the cell range A1 to I18.

The location (or 'address') of a cell is given by its column letter and row number, e.g. the cell at the intersection of the second column and the fifth row (as here) is given the address or cell reference B5.

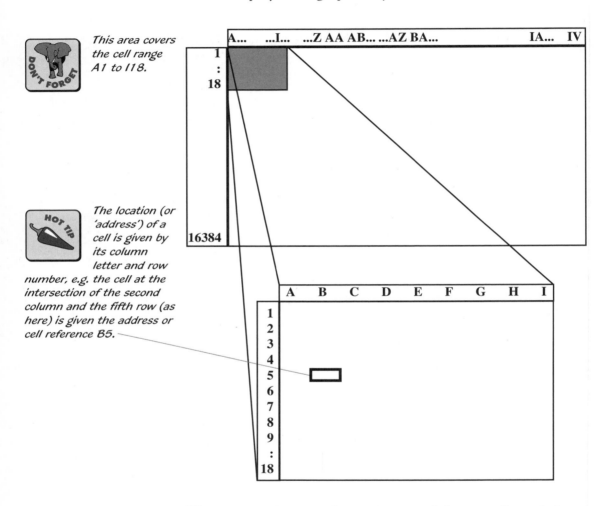

The grey section – only a tiny part of the overall worksheet – is shown in its overall context in the lower half of the illustration.

Keying in data

Note that Excel 2000 supports Year 2000 date formats. This means, for instance, that '12th December 2000' appears (by default) as:

12/12/00

(the precise format may vary).

In Excel 2000, you can enter the following basic data types:

* values (i.e. numbers)

* text (e.g. headings and explanatory material)

* functions (e.g. Sine or Cosine)

* formulas (combinations of values, text and functions)

You can use two techniques to enter data into any cell in a worksheet.

Entering data directly

Excel 2000 lets you insert and work with Euros. To insert the Euro symbol, hold down Alt and type the following on the Numerical keypad to the right of your keyboard:

0128

Finally, release Alt.

First, move the mouse pointer over any cell and left-click once. Alternatively, you can also use the keyboard to target a cell: simply move the cell pointer with the cursor keys until it's over the relevant cell.

Whichever method you use, Excel 2000 surrounds the active cell with a border.

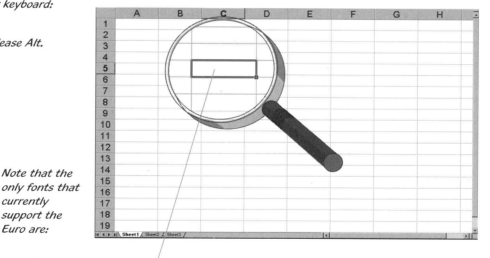

Note that the only fonts that currently support the Euro are:

* Courier
* Tahoma
* Times
* Arial

Magnified view of active cell

When you enter values which are too big (physically) to fit in the holding cell, Excel 2000 may insert an error message.

To resolve this, pull down the Format menu and click Column, Autofit Selection to have Excel automatically increase the column size to match the contents.

Now begin to key in the information required. It will appear simultaneously in the cell and in the Formula Bar.

... and in the Formula bar

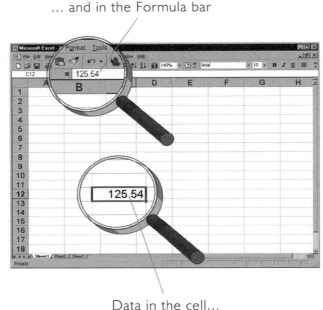

Data in the cell...

Finally, press Enter to confirm entry of the data (or Esc to cancel the operation).

Entering data via the Formula bar

You can use a keyboard route to confirm operations in the Formula bar: simply press Enter.

Click the cell you want to insert data into. Then click the Formula Bar. Type in the data. Then follow step 1 below. If you decide not to proceed with the operation, follow step 2 instead:

Click the tick

2 Click the cross

Selection techniques

Excel 2000 uses See-Through Selection – selected cells (except the first) are lightly shaded, so that you can see the result of any changes you make to underlying data.

Before you can carry out any editing operations on cells in Excel 2000, you have to select them first. Selecting a single cell is very easy: you merely click in it (we examined this on page 17). However, Excel provides a variety of selection techniques which you can use to select more than one cell.

1. Selecting adjacent cell ranges

The easiest way to do this is to use the mouse. Click in the first cell in the range; hold down the left mouse button and drag over the remaining cells. Release the mouse button.

You can use the keyboard, too. Select the first cell in the range. Hold down one Shift key as you use the relevant cursor key to extend the selection. Release the keys when the correct selection has been defined.

Re 1. – you can use another keyboard route. Place the cell pointer in the first cell. Press F8 – the following appears in the Status bar at the base of the screen:

2. Selecting separate cell ranges

Excel lets you select more than one range at a time. Look at the illustration below:

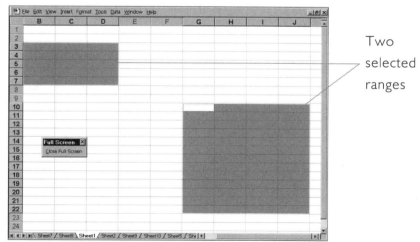

Two selected ranges

Shows that Excel is in Selection mode

Use the cursor keys to define the selection. Finally, press F8 again.

To select joint ranges, select the first in the normal way (you can only use the mouse method here). Then hold down Ctrl as you select subsequent ranges.

Groups of adjacent cells are known as 'ranges' in Excel.

Ranges are described in terms of their upper-left and lower-right cell references (with each separated by a colon).

For example, the range beginning with cell D3 and ending with H16 would be shown as:

D3:H16

3. Selecting a single row or column

To select every cell within a row or column automatically, click the row or column heading.

Column heading

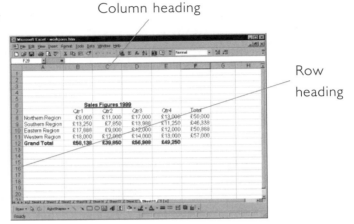

Row heading

Non-adjacent ranges are separated by commas e.g.: A3:B9,D3:H16

4. Selecting multiple rows or columns

To select more than one row or column, click a row or column heading. Hold down the left mouse button and drag to select adjacent rows or columns.

5. Selecting an entire worksheet

Carry out step 1 below:

Click the Select All button

You can use a keyboard shortcut to select every cell automatically. Simply press Ctrl+A.

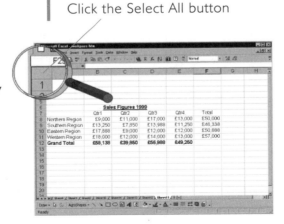

Moving around in worksheets

Excel 2000 worksheets are huge. Moving to cells which happen to be visible is easy: you simply click in the relevant cell. However, Excel provides several techniques you can use to jump to less accessible areas.

When you carry out method 1 on the right, Excel displays a bubble showing where you're up to:

Row: 15

Using the scroll bars

Use any of the following methods:

1. to scroll quickly to another section of the active worksheet, drag the scroll box along the scroll bar until you reach it

2. to move one window to the right or left, click to the left or right of the scroll box in the horizontal scroll bar

3. to move one window up or down, click above or below the scroll box in the vertical scroll bar

When you carry out method 1 in respect of especially large worksheets, hold down one Shift key at the same time to speed up the operation.

4. to move up or down by one row, click the arrows in the vertical scroll bar

5. to move left or right by one column, click the arrows in the horizontal scroll bar

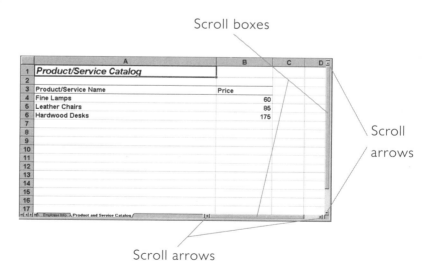

Scroll boxes

Scroll arrows

Scroll arrows

...cont'd

Excel 2000 facilitates worksheet navigation. As you move the insertion point from cell to cell, the relevant row and column headers are emboldened:

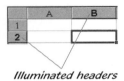

Illuminated headers

You can use a keyboard shortcut to launch this dialog. Simply press F5 or Ctrl+G.

Using the keyboard

You can use the following techniques:

1. use the cursor keys to move one cell left, right, up or down

2. hold down Ctrl as you use 1. above; this jumps to the edge of the current section (e.g. if cell B11 is active and you hold down Ctrl as you press ➝, Excel jumps to IV11, the last cell in row 11)

3. press Home to jump to the first cell in the active row, or Ctrl+Home to move to A1

4. press Page Up or Page Down to move up or down by one screen

5. press Alt+Page Down to move one screen to the right, or Alt+Page Up to move one screen to the left

Using the Go To dialog

Excel 2000 provides a special dialog which you can use to specify precise cell destinations.

Pull down the Edit menu and click Go To. Now do the following:

Re step 1 – a cell's 'reference' (or 'address') identifies it in relation to its position in a worksheet, e.g. B11 or H23. You can also type in cell ranges here.

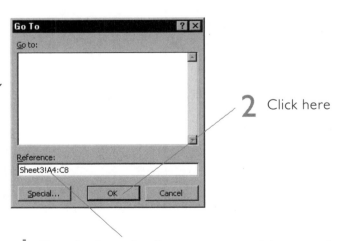

2 Click here

1 Type in the cell reference you want to move to

Switching between worksheets

Because workbooks have more than one worksheet, Excel 2000 provides two easy and convenient methods for moving between them.

See page 8 if you're not sure how to find the Tab area.

Using the Tab area

You can use the Tab area (at the base of the Excel screen) to:

- jump to the first or last sheet

- jump to the next or previous sheet

- jump to a specific sheet

See the illustration below:

When you click a worksheet tab, Excel 2000 emboldens the name and makes the tab background white.

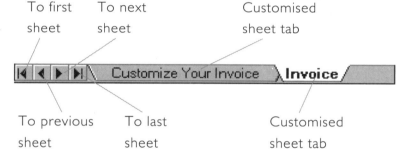

To move to a specific sheet, simply click the relevant tab.

An example: in the illustration above, to jump to the 'Customize Your Invoice' worksheet, simply click the appropriate tab.

Using the keyboard

You can use keyboard shortcuts here:

Ctrl+Page Up   moves to the previous tab/sheet

Ctrl+Page Down   moves to the next tab/sheet

Using Excel 2000's HELP system

Excel 2000 supports the standard Windows HELP system. For instance:

- Moving the mouse pointer over toolbar buttons produces an explanatory HELP bubble:

- You can move the mouse pointer over fields in dialogs, commands or screen areas and produce a specific HELP box. Carry out the following procedure to achieve this:

Excel 2000 calls these highly specific HELP bubbles 'ScreenTips'.

Right-click a field and left-click the box which launches...

Displays Help text, explaining what the command does.

...to produce a specific HELP topic

Other standard Windows HELP features are also present; see your Windows documentation for how to use these. Additionally, Excel 2000 has inbuilt HELP in the normal way...

Excel 2000 also has one further HELP feature: the Office Assistant. See the next topic.

The Office Assistant

Excel 2000 has a unique HELP feature which is designed to make it much easier to become productive: the Office Assistant. The Assistant:

- answers questions directly. This is an especially useful feature for the reason that, normally when you invoke a program's HELP system, you know more or less the question you want to ask, or the topic on which you need information. If neither of these is true, however, the Office Assistant responds to plain English questions and provides a choice of answers. For example, responses produced by entering 'What are ScreenTips?' include:

  — *Ways to get assistance while you work*

  — *Show or hide toolbar ScreenTips*

  — *Rename a menu command or toolbar button*

- offers HELP which relates specifically to Excel 2000

- provides context-sensitive tips

- answers questions phrased in your own words

The Office Assistant is animated. It can also change shape!
To achieve this, click the Options button. In the dialog which appears, activate the Gallery tab. Click the Next button until the Assistant you want is displayed. Click OK, then follow any further on-screen instructions.

If the HELP bubble isn't displayed, simply click anywhere in the Assistant:

The Excel 2000 Office Assistant, after it has just launched

...cont'd

You can also use a keyboard shortcut to launch the Office Assistant. Simply press F1.

Launching the Office Assistant

By default, the Office Assistant displays automatically. If it isn't currently on-screen, however, refer to the Standard toolbar and do the following:

Click here

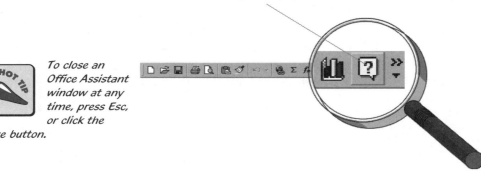

To close an Office Assistant window at any time, press Esc, or click the Close button.

Hiding the Office Assistant

If you want to hide the Office Assistant temporarily , right-click over it and do the following:

If you don't want to use the Office Assistant at all, do the following.

Click here:
In the Office Assistant dialog, activate the Options tab. Deselect Use the Office Assistant. Click OK.

Click here

...cont'd

Spontaneous tips

Sometimes, the Office Assistant will indicate that it has a tip which may be useful. Carry out the following procedures:

As you'll have noticed, you can change the Assistant. For how to do this, see the HOT TIP on page 25.

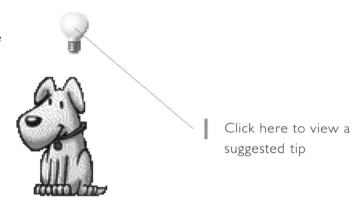

| Click here to view a suggested tip

The tip launches. Do the following when you've finished with it:

To turn the Assistant back on after you've disabled it, pull down the Help menu and do the following:

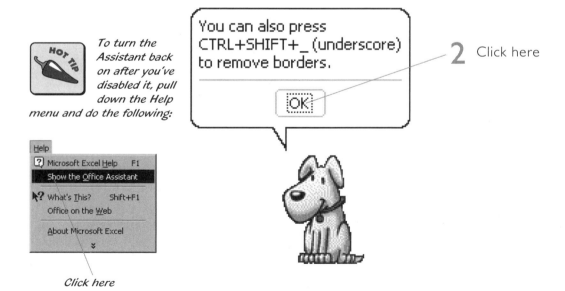

2 Click here

Click here

If the Assistant doesn't provide the right answer, you can send your query to a special Web site with more information.

Ensure your Internet connection is live, then do the following:

You can use the Office Assistant (whatever its current incarnation) to ask questions in plain English. This is of considerable benefit: you can use the Assistant to find information on topics which you aren't sure how to classify.

Asking questions

First, ensure the Office Assistant is visible. Then do the following:

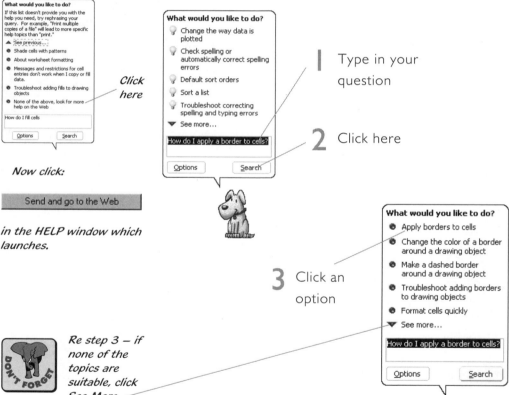

Click here

Now click:

Send and go to the Web

in the HELP window which launches.

| Type in your question

2 Click here

3 Click an option

Re step 3 – if none of the topics are suitable, click See More for a further selection. (But see the tip above for access to even more answers.)

Excel now launches a separate HELP window to one side of the screen, with the selected topic displayed. (Links to further topics may also display – click one to activate it).

When you've finished using the HELP window, click this button – ✕ – in the far right-hand corner.

Quick File Switching

Note that to use Quick File Switching you need the following:

- *Windows 98 (or a later version), or;*
- *Windows 95 with Internet Explorer 4.0 (or higher)*

In the past, only programs (not individual windows within programs) displayed on the Windows Taskbar. With Excel 2000, however, all open windows display as separate buttons.

In the following example, four new documents have been created in Excel 2000. All four display as separate windows, although only one copy of Excel 2000 is running:

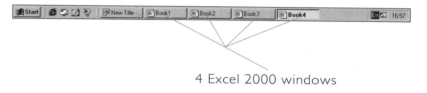

4 Excel 2000 windows

To begin a discussion (see page 30 for how to pre-select a server), open a workbook. Pull down the Tools menu and click Online Collaboration, Web Discussions. Click the Discussions button in the toolbar at the base of the screen; select Insert about the Workbook. Complete the dialog and click OK – the Discussion pane launches.

(To reply to a discussion, click Show a menu of actions, then Reply. Type your answer under Discussion text.)

This is clarified by a glance at Excel 2000's Window menu which (as with previous versions) shows all open Excel windows:

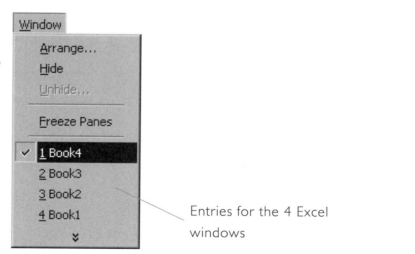

Entries for the 4 Excel windows

Use this technique to go to a workbook window by simply clicking its Taskbar button – a considerable saving in time and effort.

Repairing errors

If Office Server Extensions have been installed on your server, you can add discussions to Excel 2000 worksheets (including HTML files) stored on it.

To select a server, ensure your Internet connection is live. Then pull down the Tools menu and click Online Collaboration, Web Discussions. The Discussion Options dialog appears. (If it doesn't, click the Discussions button in the toolbar at the base of the screen and select Discussion Options in the menu.)

Click Add. Complete the Add or Edit Discussion Servers dialog. Click OK twice.

(To start a discussion, see the DON'T FORGET tip on page 29.)

Excel 2000 provides the following:

Automatic repair

Whenever you launch Excel 2000, it:

1. determines if essential files are missing or corrupted

2. automatically reinstalls the files

3. repairs incorrect entries (relating to missing or corrupted files) in the Windows Registry

Manual repair

There are other potential problems which, though far less serious, can still result in lost productivity – e.g. corrupted fonts and missing templates.

Excel 2000 has a special diagnostic procedure (called 'Detect and Repair') which you can run when necessary. The procedure:

1. scrutinises the original state of your installation

2. compares this with the present state of your installation

3. takes the appropriate remedial steps

To run Detect and Repair, pull down the Help menu and do the following:

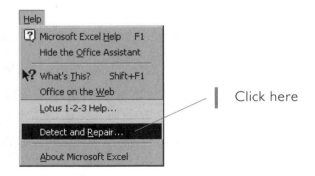

Click here

Excel 2000 now detects and remedies any problem – this process may take some time.

Worksheet basics

In this chapter, you'll learn how to 'forward-plan' worksheets, to ensure your data is easy to follow. We'll also examine the different types of data you can enter, and look at how to modify data you've already entered. Excel 2000 has several features which act as shortcuts to data entry; you'll use these to save time and effort. Then you'll discover how to work with number formats; specify suitable data types; insert formulas into cells; and carry out simple What-If tests. Finally, you'll resize rows and columns, and insert new cells, rows and columns.

Covers

Chapter Two

Layout planning

As you enter data into your worksheet, use the techniques discussed here (and on page 45) to ensure your data is clear and easily comprehensible.

You should also ensure your worksheet has an effective overall 'look' – see Chapter 12 for more information on how to format worksheets.

When you start Excel 2000, a blank worksheet is automatically created and loaded. This means you can click any cell and start entering data immediately. However, it's a good idea to give some thought to an overall layout strategy before you do this.

Look at the simple worksheet excerpt below:

2		Widgets ordered =	425
3		Price per unit =	0.73
4		Amount due (excluding VAT) =	

Here, the text occupies far more space than the numbers and formulas. The problem has been solved by widening the column containing the text (see page 45 for how to do this). The problem is that this method prevents subsequent lines in the column from being subdivided into further columns.

Look at the next illustration:

2		Widgets ordered =		425
3		Price per unit =		0.73
4		Amount due (excluding VAT) =		

This text has bled into the next column

The second method is often the most flexible.

Here, on the other hand, the final text entry has been allowed to straddle as many adjacent columns as necessary. The proviso here is that you must ensure you leave as many empty adjacent cells as are necessary fully to display the text.

Data types

To force a sequence of digits to be input as text, precede them by a single quotation mark. For instance, to type in 1234 as text type:

'1234

In Chapter 1 (pages 17-18), we looked at how to key in simple data. Now, we'll examine the types of data you can enter in more detail.

Excel 2000 determines the type of data entered into a cell by the sequence of characters keyed. The types are:

- numbers (i.e. digits, decimal point, #, %, +, −)

- text (any other string of characters)

- formulas (always preceded by =)

The worksheet excerpt below shows these data types in action:

These are default alignments. To apply a new alignment, select the cell(s). Right-click over them. In the menu, click Format Cells. In the Format Cells dialog, click the Alignment tab. Select a new alignment. Click OK.

B2 contains text (aligned to the left of the cell)

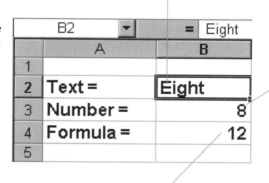

B3 contains the number 8 (aligned to the right of the cell)

B4 contains the hidden formula: =8+4

If you want to display the underlying formula rather than the result, select the relevant cell and press:

Ctrl+'

(The ' character is at the top left of the keyboard, below the function keys.)

When a formula has been inserted into a cell, Excel 2000 evaluates it. The resultant value – in the case of B4 above, 12 – is shown, aligned to the right.

For more information on formulas, see pages 42-43.

Modifying existing data

To undo one or more editing actions, you should do carry out the following procedure:

— *Click here*

in the Standard toolbar. Make your selection in the list but note that, if you select an early operation (i.e. one near the bottom), all later operations are included.

You can amend the contents of a cell in two ways:

•   via the Formula bar

•   from within the cell

When you use either of these methods, Excel 2000 enters a special state known as Edit Mode.

Amending existing data using the Formula Bar

Click the cell whose contents you want to change. Then click in the Formula bar. Make the appropriate revisions and/or additions. Then press Enter. Excel updates the relevant cell.

Amending existing data internally

Click the cell whose contents you want to change. Press F2. Make the appropriate revisions and/or additions *within the cell*. Then press Enter.

To redo one or more editing actions, you should carry out the following procedure:

— *Click here*

in the Standard toolbar. Make your selection in the list, but see the caveat in the tip above.

(If you haven't used Redo lately, or if you've expanded the Formatting toolbar, the button above may be in the fly-out – click » to launch it.)

The illustration below shows a section from a simple Excel workbook:

A magnified view of a cell in Edit Mode (note the flashing insertion point)

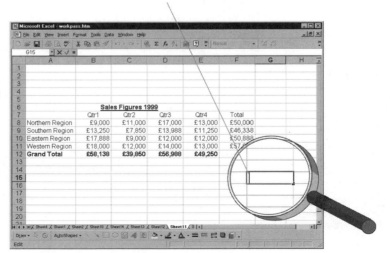

AutoComplete

If in-cell editing (see page 34) doesn't work, pull down the Tools menu and click Options. Select the Edit tab, then click 'Edit directly in cell'. Finally, click OK.

Excel 2000 has a range of features which save you time and effort:

- AutoComplete

- AutoFill

- AutoCorrect

AutoComplete examines the contents of the active column and tries to anticipate what you're about to type. Look at the next illustration:

You can also use another technique. Instead of starting to type in the repeat entry, right-click over the cell. In the menu, click Pick From List. Now do the following:

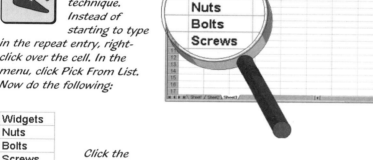

Here, we've entered a series of text values into cells B4:B7. If you want to duplicate any of these entries in B8, you can (in this instance) simply type in the first letter then press Enter.

Click the entry you want to use

Use the example here as a guide – you may have to enter more than one letter...

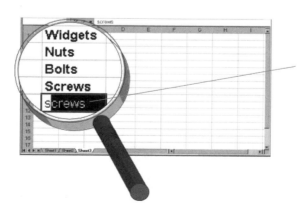

Typing in 's' has prompted Excel 2000 to insert the correct term...

AutoFill

Excel 2000 lets you insert data series automatically. This is a very useful feature. Look at the illustration below:

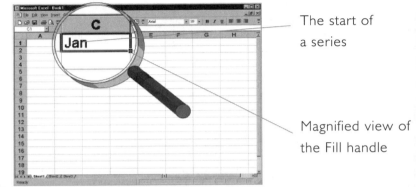

The start of a series

Magnified view of the Fill handle

If you wanted to insert month names in successive cells in column C, you could do so manually. But there's a much easier way. You can use Excel's AutoFill feature.

Using AutoFill to create a series

Type in the first element(s) of the series in consecutive cells. Select all the cells. Then position the mouse pointer over the Fill handle in the bottom right-hand corner of the last cell (the pointer changes to a crosshair). Hold down the left mouse button and drag the handle over the cells into which you want to extend the series (in the example above, over C2:C12). When you release the mouse button, Excel 2000 extrapolates the initial entry or entries into the appropriate series.

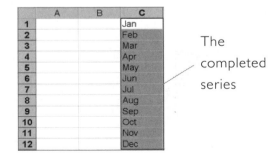

The completed series

AutoCorrect – an overview

AutoCorrect is a very useful Excel 2000 feature. Its principal purpose is to correct typing errors automatically. It does this by maintaining a list of inaccurate spellings and their corrected versions. When you press the Spacebar or Enter/ Return keys immediately after making an error, the correction is substituted for the original error.

AutoCorrect is supplied with a long list of preset corrections. The following are examples:

- allwasy becomes always

- acomodate becomes accommodate

- alot becomes a lot

- do'nt becomes don't

- garantee becomes guarantee

- oppertunity becomes opportunity

- wierd becomes weird

In addition, however, you can easily define your own. If, for instance, you regularly type 'lthe' when you mean 'the', you can have AutoCorrect make the correction for you.

You can also enter shortened forms of correct words – or entire phrases – and have them expanded automatically. (For instance, you could have AutoCorrect expand 'ann' into 'Annual Profit Forecast'...)

AutoCorrect has further uses. You can have:

1.   the first letters of sentences capitalised

2.   words which begin with two capitals corrected (e.g. 'HEllo' becomes 'Hello')

3.   days capitalised (e.g. 'monday' becomes 'Monday')

Customising AutoCorrect

You can add new corrections, delete existing ones or specify which AutoCorrect functions are active.

Adding new corrections

Pull down the Tools menu and do the following:

Re step 1 – the relevant entry on your menu may currently be hidden if you haven't used AutoCorrect before.

If it is, wait a few seconds then follow step 1.

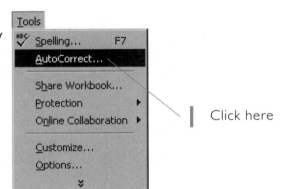

| Click here

If you don't want errors corrected automatically, deselect Replace text as you type.

2 Type in the incorrect word

3 Type in the correction

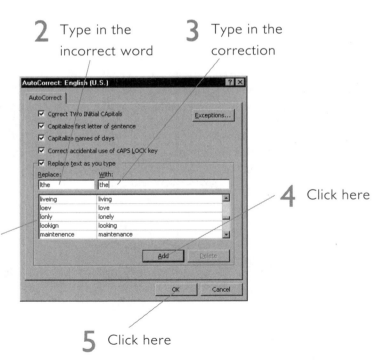

4 Click here

To remove an entry, first select it here: Now click the following

button:

Delete

Excel 2000 deletes the item immediately.

5 Click here

Setting other AutoCorrect options

Perform step 1 on page 38. Now do the following:

An exception is a letter or word (followed by a full stop) after which you don't want to capitalise the first letter of the following word.

2 Click any of these options to deselect them

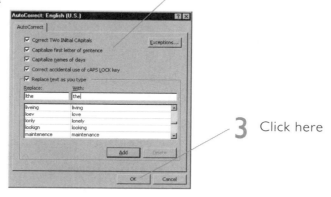

3 Click here

Ensure the First Letter tab is active before you carry out steps A-C.

Specifying exceptions

There are situations where Excel's automatic capitalisation is wrong. For instance, if you type in 'approx.' followed by another word, the first letter of the second word is capitalised due to the preceding full stop, which may not be what you want. To prevent this, you can set up an exception.

This dialog does not distinguish between lower- and upper-case. For example, entering 'quart.' has the same effect as entering 'Quart.'.

In the above dialog, click this button –  – and do the following:

A Type in an exception

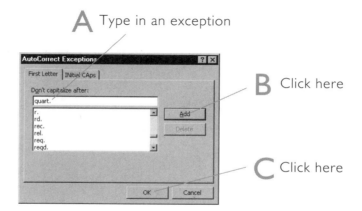

B Click here

C Click here

After step C, carry out step 3 above.

Number formats

You can customise the way cell contents (e.g. numbers and dates/times) display in Excel 2000. You can specify:

- at what point numbers are rounded up

- how minus values are displayed (for example, whether they display in red, and/or with '–' in front of them)

- (in the case of currency values) which currency symbol (e.g. £ or $) is used

- (in the case of dates and times) the generic display type (e.g. *day/month/year* or *month/year*)

Available formats are organised under general categories. These include: Number, Currency and Fraction.

Specifying a number format

Select the cells whose contents you want to customise. Pull down the Format menu and click Cells. Now do the following:

Re step 3 – the options you can choose from vary according to the category chosen. Complete them as necessary.

1 Ensure the Number tab is active

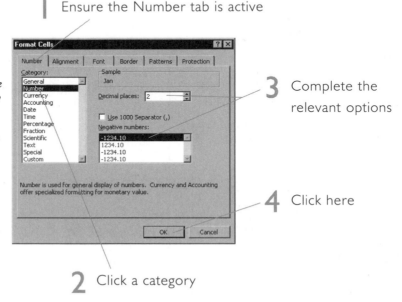

3 Complete the relevant options

4 Click here

2 Click a category

Data validation

To apply a character limit, select Text Length in step 3. Follow step 4. In step 5, enter min. and max. limits (e.g. '4' and '8'). Carry out step 6.

You can have Excel 2000 'validate' data. This can mean:

- restricting cells so only data which is within specific limits (numerical or temporal) can be entered

- restricting cells so only a specific number of characters can be entered

Applying data validation

Select one or more cells. Pull down the Data menu and do the following:

Re step 5 – depending on the type of limit imposed in step 3, you can enter:

- *values*
- *formulas*
- *cell addresses*

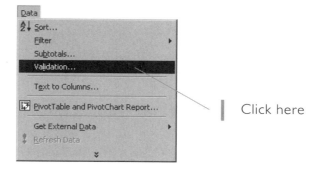

1 Click here

Re step 4 – you can select from the following operators:

- *between*
- *not between*
- *equal to*
- *not equal to*
- *greater than*
- *less than*
- *greater than or equal to*
- *less than or equal to*

(The dialog changes according to which is chosen.)

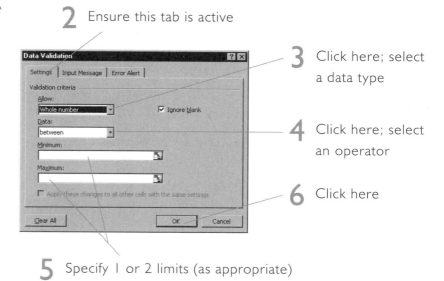

2 Ensure this tab is active

3 Click here; select a data type

4 Click here; select an operator

6 Click here

5 Specify 1 or 2 limits (as appropriate)

Formulas – an overview

Formulas are cell entries which define how other values relate to each other.

As a very simple example, consider the following:

For brief details of frequently used formulas, do the following.

Click the Office Assistant. In the HELP box, type in: formulas, examples then press Enter.

Now click 'Examples of commonly used formulas' in the list of topics. Excel 2000 launches a HELP window giving examples of common formulas.

When you've finished using this, click:

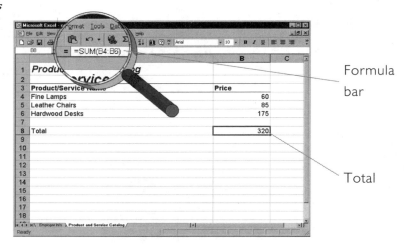

Formula bar

Total

in the top right hand corner of the HELP window.

Here, a cell (B8) has been defined which returns the total of cells B4:B6. Obviously, in this instance you could insert the total easily enough yourself because the individual values are so small, and because we're only dealing with a small number of cells. But what happens if the cell values are larger and/or more numerous, or – more to the point – if they're liable to change frequently?

The answer is to insert a formula which carries out the necessary calculation automatically.

If you look at the Formula bar in the illustration, you'll see the formula which does this:

=SUM(B4:B6)

Many Excel 2000 formulas are more complex than this, but the principles remain the same.

Inserting a formula

Arguments (e.g. cell references) relating to functions are always bracketed.

To enter the same formula into a cell range, select the range, type the formula and then press Ctrl+Enter.

If you want to revise a formula, you can also use a feature known as Range Finder.

Double-click the cell which contains the formula; Excel applies a separate colour to each cell range referred to in the formula. Drag the relevant coloured border to restate the formula reference (or drag the border handle to extend or reduce it).

Finally, press Enter.

All formulas in Excel 2000 begin with an equals sign. This is usually followed by a permutation of the following:

- an operand (cell reference, e.g. B4)

- a function (e.g. the summation function, SUM)

- an arithmetical operator ($+$, $-$, $/$ and $*$)

- comparison operators ($<$, $>$, $<=$, $>=$ and $=$)

Excel supports a very wide range of functions organised into numerous categories. (For more information on how to insert functions, see chapter 6.)

The mathematical operators are (in the order in which they appear in the list): *plus*, *minus*, *divide* and *multiply*.

The comparison operators are (in the order in which they appear in the list): *less than*, *greater than*, *less than or equal to*, *greater than or equal to* and *equals*.

There are two ways to enter formulas:

Entering a formula directly into the cell

Click the cell in which you want to insert a formula. Then type = followed by your formula. When you've finished, press Enter.

Entering a formula into the Formula bar

This is usually the most convenient method.

Click the cell in which you want to insert a formula. Then click in the Formula bar. Type = followed by your formula. When you've finished, press Enter or do the following:

Click here

Simple What-If tests

The power of a worksheet is only really appreciated when you carry out 'What-If' tests. These involve adjusting the numbers in selected cells in order to observe the effect on formulas throughout the worksheet. Any such changes 'ripple through' the worksheet.

In the simple example below, C4 has the following formula:

$=C2*C3$

which multiplies the contents of C2 by C3.

	A	B	C
1			
2		Widgets ordered =	425
3		Price per unit =	0.73
4		Amount due (excluding VAT) =	310.25

If changes you make to data don't produce the relevant update, pull down the Tools menu and click Options. In the Options dialog, select the Calculation tab. Click Automatic in the Calculation section, followed by OK.

By entering alternative values into C2 or C3, you can watch the changes filter through to C4. In the next illustration, the value in C2 has changed; Excel 2000 has automatically calculated the effect on the total:

	A	B	C
1			
2		Widgets ordered =	562
3		Price per unit =	0.73
4		Amount due (excluding VAT) =	410.26

The change in C2 has automatically adjusted the C4 total

Amending row/column sizes

Sooner or later, you'll find it necessary to resize rows or columns. This necessity arises when there is too much data in cells to display adequately. You can enlarge or shrink single or multiple rows/columns.

Changing row height

To change one row's height, click the row heading. If you want to change multiple rows, hold down Ctrl and click the appropriate extra headings. Then place the mouse pointer (it changes to a cross) just under the row heading(s). Hold down the left mouse button and drag up or down to decrease or increase the row(s) respectively. Release the mouse button to confirm the operation.

Excel has a useful 'Best Fit' feature. When the mouse pointer has changed to:

double-click to have the row(s) or column(s) adjust themselves automatically to their contents.

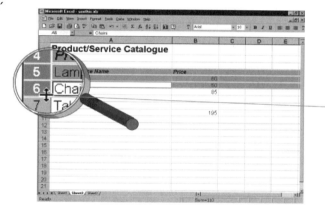

A magnified view of the transformed pointer – here, we're amending rows 4, 5 and 6 jointly

Changing column width

To change one column's width, click the column heading. If you want to change multiple columns, hold down Ctrl and click the appropriate extra headings. Then place the mouse pointer (it changes to a cross) just to the right of the column heading(s). Hold down the left mouse button and drag right or left to widen or narrow the column(s) respectively.

Release the mouse button to confirm the operation.

Inserting cells, rows or columns

You can insert additional cells, rows or columns into worksheets.

Inserting a new row or column

First, select one or more cells within the row(s) or column(s) where you want to carry out the insert operation. Now pull down the Insert menu and click Rows or Columns, as appropriate. Excel 2000 inserts the new row(s) or column(s) immediately.

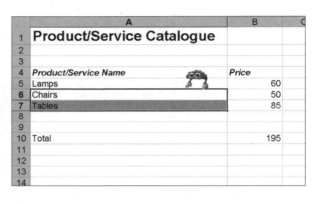

	A	B	C
1	**Product/Service Catalogue**		
2			
3			
4	*Product/Service Name*	Price	
5	Lamps	60	
6	Chairs	50	
7	Tables	85	
8			
9			
10	Total	195	
11			
12			
13			
14			

Here, one new column or two new rows are being added

Inserting a new cell range

Select the range where you want to insert the new cells. Pull down the Insert menu and click Cells. Now carry out step 1 or step 2 below. Finally, follow step 3.

1 Click here to have Excel make room for the new cells by moving the selected range to the right

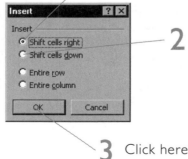

2 Click here to have Excel make room for the new cells by moving the selected range down

3 Click here

Copy/move techniques

In this chapter, you'll learn how to copy and move cells. You'll copy/move data within the host worksheet, to another worksheet and to another (open) workbook. You'll also perform copy operations which are restricted to specific cell aspects, then make use of a shortcut which makes copying data to *adjacent* cells even easier. You'll also perform multiple copy operations with Excel 2000's native Clipboard, then move worksheets to a different location within the host workbook (and to another workbook).

Finally, you'll drag-and-drop data directly into Excel 2000 from within Internet Explorer.

Covers

Chapter Three

Copying and moving cells

See also page 52 for how to use AutoFill to copy cell data.

Excel 2000 lets you copy or move cells:

- within the same worksheet (see pages 48–50)

- from one worksheet to another (see page 51)

- from one worksheet to another worksheet in a different workbook (see page 51)

Copying data within the same worksheet

Select the cell range which contains the data you want to copy. Move the mouse pointer over the range border; it changes to an arrow. Hold down one Ctrl key; left-click and drag the range to the new location. Release the mouse button.

When you copy or move data in cells which contain formulas, Excel adjusts the cell references.

Cells in the course of being copied

When you perform a copy operation, the mouse pointer looks like this:

In a move operation, on the other hand, it looks like this:

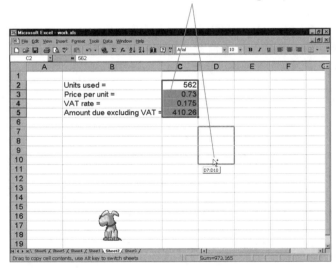

Moving data within the same worksheet

Select the cell range which contains the data you want to move. Place the mouse pointer over the range border; it changes to an arrow. Left-click and drag the range to the new location. Release the mouse button.

Advanced copying

Re step 1 – if you haven't used it much (or if you've expanded the Formatting toolbar), the Copy button may be on the Standard toolbar fly-out instead. If it is, click:

to access it.

Excel 2000 allows you to be highly specific about which cell components are copied. You can use a special technique to limit the copy operation to any of the following (but only one at a time):

- the cell format

- underlying formulas

- cell values

- any data validation rules you've set

- all cell contents and formats

Performing specific copy operations

Select the data you want to copy. Then refer to the Standard toolbar and do the following:

Click the Copy button

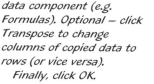

After step 2, pull down the Edit menu and click Paste Special. In the Paste Special dialog, select a data component (e.g. Formulas). Optional – click Transpose to change columns of copied data to rows (or vice versa). Finally, click OK.

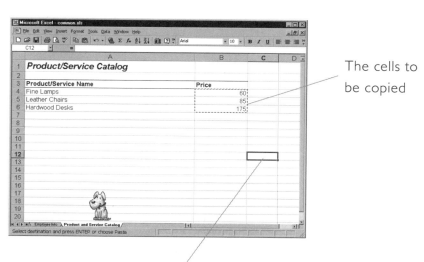

The cells to be copied

2 Click the upper left cell in the Paste Area (the cell range into which you want the data copied)

Collect and Paste

The Clipboard is a memory area where copied data is stored until it is pasted into another worksheet.

In Excel 2000, you can also use standard Windows copying techniques:

A.   Ctrl+C copies selected cell data

B.   Ctrl+X copies and deletes (i.e. 'moves') selected cell data

C.   Ctrl+V inserts ('pastes in') the copied data

Using Collect and Paste, you can store as many as 12 items at once.

These techniques use the standard Windows Clipboard to store the data. However, there is one major disadvantage: you can only store one item at a time. Fortunately, Excel 2000 lets you avoid this limitation. You can:

- copy/move multiple items of data

To paste in all current Clipboard items, carry out the following procedure. Click:

- paste in multiple items of data

using a special Excel Clipboard. Excel 2000 calls this feature 'Collect and Paste'.

Using Collect and Paste

(if available).

Copy or move the first item, using A. or B. respectively above. As soon as you copy/move the second, Excel 2000 launches its Clipboard toolbar. Continue copying/moving items, as required. When you're ready to paste them in, do the following:

Select the cell(s) where you want to insert the data

To see what a Clipboard item relates to, hold the mouse pointer over it – an explanatory bubble appears.

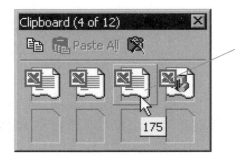

2 Click a
Clipboard item

To close the Excel 2000 Clipboard, click this button:

Repeat steps 1–2 as often as necessary.

External copy/move operations

You can easily copy or move a range of cells between worksheets and workbooks.

Moving data to another Worksheet

When you move the mouse pointer over the appropriate tab,

Excel highlights it:

Drag the cell range back into the worksheet area (the second worksheet is now displayed) and position it in the correct location.

Select the cell range which contains the data you want to move. Place the mouse pointer over the range border; it changes to an arrow. Hold down the Alt key; left-click and drag the range onto the relevant worksheet tab:

The Worksheet tab area at the base of the screen

Position the range using the techniques discussed in the upper DON'T FORGET tip.

Copying data to another Worksheet

If you manually close the Clipboard toolbar (see the facing page) without pasting in any data, selecting multiple data items will no longer make it appear.

To rectify this, pull down the Tools menu and click Toolbar, Clipboard.

Select the cell range which contains the data you want to copy. Place the mouse pointer over the range border; it changes to an arrow. Hold down the Alt key and one Ctrl key; left-click and drag the range onto the relevant worksheet tab, then position it using the techniques discussed in the DON'T FORGET tip.

Moving data to another Workbook

First open both workbooks in separate windows (for how to do this, see your Windows documentation). Select the cell range which contains the data you want to move. Place the mouse pointer over the range border; it changes to an arrow. Left-click and drag the range onto the relevant worksheet in the second workbook.

Before you move/copy data to another workbook, pre-select the appropriate worksheet.

Copying data to another Workbook

First open both workbooks in separate windows. Select the cell range containing the data to be copied. Place the mouse pointer over the border; it changes to an arrow. Hold down one Ctrl key; left-click and drag the range onto the relevant worksheet in the second workbook.

Entering data automatically

On page 36, we looked at the use of AutoFill to extrapolate data from one or more cells into additional cells. You can also use a variant of AutoFill to make copying data easier.

If you're using this technique to copy the contents of more than one cell, and you don't hold down one Ctrl key as you drag, Excel 2000 will extrapolate (rather than copy) the data.

Copying data to adjacent cells – a shortcut

Select the cell range which contains the data you want to copy.

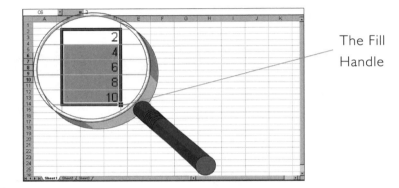

The Fill Handle

If you're using this technique to copy the contents of a single cell, don't hold down Ctrl.
(If you do, Excel will extrapolate – rather than copy – the data.)

Move the mouse pointer over the Fill Handle. Hold down one Ctrl key; left-click and drag the handle over as many adjacent cells as you want to copy the data into. Release the mouse pointer to confirm the copy operation:

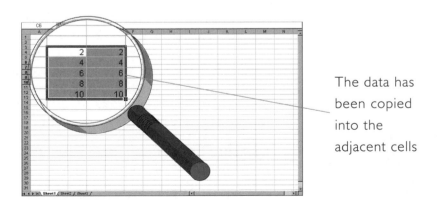

The data has been copied into the adjacent cells

Moving worksheets

To insert a new worksheet, click the tab (in the tab area) which represents the sheet in front of which you want the new worksheet inserted. (To insert multiple sheets, hold down Ctrl and click the relevant number of tabs.)

Finally, pull down the Insert menu and click Worksheet.

You can perform two kinds of move operation on worksheets. You can:

• rearrange the worksheet order within a given workbook

• transfer a worksheet to another workbook

Rearranging worksheets

To select a single worksheet, click the relevant sheet tab in the Worksheet tab area. (Or select more than one worksheet by holding down Ctrl as you click multiple tabs.) With the mouse pointer still over the selected tab(s), hold down the left mouse button and drag them to their new location in the tab area. Release the mouse button to confirm the operation.

Moving worksheets to another workbook

To select a single worksheet, click the relevant sheet tab in the worksheet tab area. (Or select more than one worksheet by holding down Ctrl as you click multiple tabs.) Pull down the Edit menu and click Move or Copy Sheet. Now do the following:

To delete a worksheet, click its tab in the tab area. Pull down the Edit menu and click Delete Sheet. In the message which launches, click OK.

(Deleting a sheet erases its contents too!)

Click here; select the new host workbook from the drop-down list

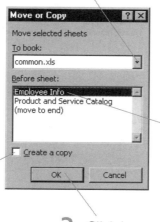

2 Click the worksheet in front of which you want the transferred sheet(s) to appear

Click here: to perform a copy operation rather than a move.

3 Click here

Copying data from Internet Explorer

To use method A, select the relevant data in Internet Explorer. Press Ctrl+C to copy it, or Ctrl+X to move it. Position the cursor at the location in Excel 2000 where you want the data inserted. Press Shift+Insert.

A special relationship exists between Excel 2000 and Internet Explorer 5. Because the Windows Clipboard now recognises the HTML file format, you can:

A. copy data from Internet Explorer and paste it into Excel

B. drag-and-drop data from Internet Explorer into Excel

Using method B.

With Excel 2000 and Internet Explorer both open in separate windows, do the following:

Select the relevant data in Internet Explorer, then drag it into Excel 2000

Re step 1 and the above tip – use the mouse to select data in Internet Explorer.

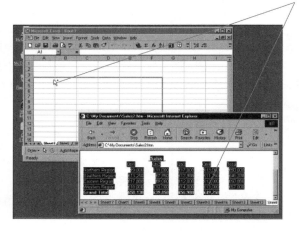

To select all data within Internet Explorer, press Ctrl+A.

2 Release the mouse button – Excel inserts the data:

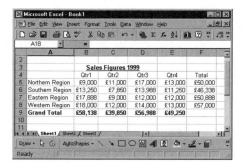

Workbook management

In this chapter, you'll learn how to create new workbooks, then save and reopen them. You'll also save workbooks as templates and as HTML files (for use on the Internet and Intranets), then have Excel 2000 save your work automatically, at an interval you set. Finally, you'll save (and reopen) your overall environment as a workspace, and then close all active workbooks.

Covers

Chapter Four

Creating new workbooks

Excel 2000 displays a preview of the selected template to the right of the dialog.

Creating new workbooks is made easy by the provision of templates. A template is a pre-designed workbook which is ready to use. The templates supplied with Excel 2000 contain:

- numerous pre-defined fields

- several pre-defined worksheets

- pre-defined formatting

- special buttons which you can click to launch features directly

Re step 1 – to create a new blank workbook, activate the General tab instead. Then omit steps 2 and 3; instead, double-click this icon:

As well as using the templates provided, you can design your own – see page 58. Alternatively you can create a new blank worksheet – see the HOT TIP.

Creating a workbook

Pull down the File menu and click New. Now do the following:

Excel 2000 creates a new workbook (with 3 blank worksheets).

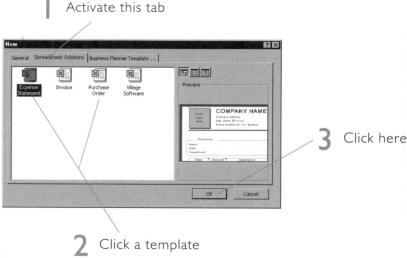

Activate this tab

3 Click here

2 Click a template

After step 3, Excel may produce a special dialog. Do the following to enable macro use:

Click here

Saving workbooks

It's important to save your work at frequent intervals, in order to avoid data loss in the event of a hardware fault or power interruption. Carry out one of the following procedures, as appropriate:

Saving a workbook for the first time

Pull down the File menu and click Save. Or press Ctrl+S. Now do the following:

Re step 2 – click any buttons here: for access to the relevant folders. (For instance, to save files to your Desktop, click Desktop.) Ignore step 3.

Repeat step 3 as necessary, until you locate the relevant folder.

2 Click here. In the drop-down list, click a drive

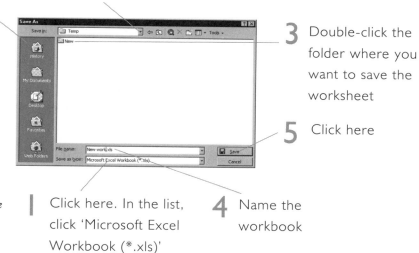

3 Double-click the folder where you want to save the worksheet

5 Click here

1 Click here. In the list, click 'Microsoft Excel Workbook (*.xls)'

4 Name the workbook

Saving a workbook which has already been saved

Pull down the File menu and click Save. Alternatively, refer to the Standard toolbar and do the following:

Click here

Saving workbooks as templates

Workbooks you've created and formatted can be saved as templates, for future use. When you've done this, you can base new documents on them (see page 56), which represents a considerable saving in time and effort.

By default, workbook templates are saved to the following folder:

\WINDOWS\Application Data\Microsoft\Templates

and appear as icons in the New dialog's General tab.

If you want to save your template to a nonstandard folder, follow step 1. Click the arrow to the right of the Save in: field. In the list, select a drive. Now double-click the necessary folder(s) here:
Finally, perform steps 2-3.

Saving a workbook as a template

Open the relevant workbook. Pull down the File menu and click Save As. Carry out the following steps:

Note that Excel 2000 templates have the suffix .XLT.

2 Name the template   3 Click here

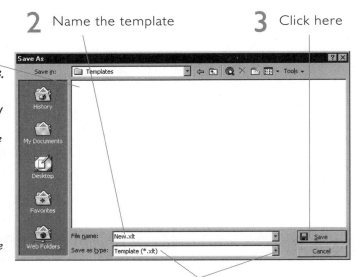

Make sure 'Template (*.xlt)' is shown.
If it isn't, click the arrow and select it
from the drop-down list

To create a Web folder (see page 59), get details of servers which support Web folders from your:

* *system administrator, or;*
* *Internet Service Provider*

Saving to the Web – an overview

You can use Explorer to create Web folders.
In the Explorer hierarchy, do the following:

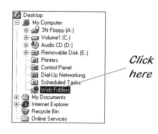

Click here

Now activate this icon in the pane on the right:

Add Web Folder

and follow the on-screen instructions.

To set up a FTP site, click Save As in the File menu. In the Save As dialog, click the Save in field. In the list, select Add/Modify FTP Locations. Complete the new dialog, then click Add. Click OK, then press Esc.

You can save workbooks (in HTML – HyperText Markup Language – format) to:

*   a pre-established Web folder (Web folders are shortcuts to Web/Intranet servers) – see the HOT TIP on the immediate left, and the DON'T FORGET tip on page 58

*   a pre-established FTP site on the World Wide Web – see the HOT TIP at the bottom of this page

You can also save HTML files directly to Intranets, using the same techniques.

Excel 2000 supports two basic types of Web page saving: interactive and non-interactive – see page 60.

HTML enhancements

While Excel 2000 workbooks preserve their own native format (*.xls) so that they're identical with the formats used by Excel 97, the standard Web format (*.html or *.htm) has had the following changes made:

*   it's now a Companion File format (Microsoft regards it as occupying the same status as its proprietary formats); this means that you can create *and* share rich Web documents with the same Excel 2000 tools used to create printed documents

*   it now duplicates the functionality of Excel 2000's own format (i.e. most Excel 2000 features are preserved when saving in HTML format)

*   you can edit HTML files from within Internet Explorer 5.0 (or higher), by clicking this button: [Edit]

    Excel 2000 automatically opens the HTML file

*   it's now recognised by the Windows Clipboard. This means that data can be copied from Internet Explorer and pasted directly into Excel 2000 – see page 54

*   from within Excel 2000, you can preview your work directly in Internet Explorer, before you've saved it to disk

Interactive v. non-interactive saving

You can save data to Web pages (on the Internet or Intranets) in two ways:

- non-interactively

- interactively

Both methods have one overriding advantage: it isn't necessary to have access to Excel 2000 in order to view the end result.

Non-interactive saving

This is the method to use if you only want users to view, not interact with, your data. Users need only have:

1. access to the Internet or an Intranet

2. any appropriate browser (e.g. Internet Explorer)

Interactive saving

There are, however, some limitations – see page 62.

Interactively means that users viewing your data can also work with it in (basically) the same way that you do in Excel 2000. For instance, they can:

- rearrange cell ranges

- update values

You can only perform interactive saves in respect of components of workbooks, not the entire workbook itself.

As with non-interactive saving, users can view interactive data in their browser, without needing to have installed Excel 2000. There are, however, additional, more stringent requirements. Users must have:

1. Internet Explorer 4.01 or later

2. access to the Office Web Components.

The Web Components are automatically installed with the Professional, Standard and Premium editions of Office 2000. Alternatively, anyone with a Microsoft Office 2000 site license can download them from an Intranet – see your network administrator for more information.

Preparing to save to the Web

There are several steps you should take before you begin any of the procedures on pages 63-65:

To publish your Excel files on the Web, you must have a live Internet connection.

1 Make sure your original Excel 2000 data is complete and correct (inc. the formatting). When you're checking your data, bear in mind the restrictions in the conversion process – see page 62. For instance, if you're planning to save a 3-D chart interactively, consider converting it to 2-D first...

2 Save the definitive version of your Excel workbook as a .XLS file, in the normal way, and keep this secure

3 Decide whether disseminating your data in .XLS format will be sufficient. This is an option if you happen to know that everyone who will view it has access to Excel 2000. If this is the case, jump to page 63 or 64, as appropriate. If it isn't, first carry out the remaining steps below

4 Decide whether you want to save to interactive or non-interactive Web pages (see page 60)

Re step 7 – if you're publishing your data in .XLS format, carry out a different procedure: select Print Preview in Excel 2000's File menu to preview it.
Press Esc when you've finished.

5 It's a good idea – before you make your data available publicly – to save a test version of your Web page on your own PC. This means you can open it in your browser and confirm that everything is as it should be. If it isn't, you can re-export your data after you've made the necessary corrections within the original Excel 2000 file (see step 2)

6 Preview the Web page (see page 63 for non-interactive previewing and the HOT TIP on page 65 for interactive previewing)

7 Decide where you want to put the Web page.

Web page conversion restrictions

The restrictions on the right apply to interactive saves – i.e. where workbook components (e.g. worksheets) are being saved for future editing.

If, however, you save an entire workbook non-interactively, the principal features which are excluded are:

- *custom views*
- *formula names*

Certain worksheet aspects either do not work – or have a different appearance – when published to a Web page. These include:

Custom views	These are not retained
Word wrap in cells	This is not retained
Data validations	These are not retained
Typefaces in cells	Only the default typeface appears (any additional typefaces you've specified do not appear)
Conditional formatting	The current cell formatting is retained but the conditionality is lost
Pictures/clip art	These do not appear
Cell comments	These are not retained
Pattern fills	These are not retained
Dotted/broken borders	These are changed to solid borders
Indented text	This is not retained
Rotated text	This is changed to horizontal text
Formula names	If you've given names to formulas (rather than references), these are converted to the appropriate references
3-D charts	These are converted to 2-D charts
Printing/page setup	These settings are not retained
R1C1 referencing	This is converted to A1 referencing

Non-interactive saving

If you want to save a workbook component non-interactively, see the DON'T FORGET tip on page 64.

Previewing your work before saving

Pull down the File menu and do the following:

Click here

Before you can save files to Web folders or FTP sites, you must first have carried out the relevant procedures in the HOT TIPS on page 59, and the DON'T FORGET tip on page 58.

Your browser now launches, with your work displayed in it. To close it when you've finished using it, press Alt+F4.

Publishing workbooks non-interactively

Pull down the File menu and click Save as Web Page. Then do the following:

Click here. In the drop-down list, select a recipient – see the HOT TIP

HOT TIP

Re step 1 – you should carry out one of the following procedures:

* *To save to a FTP site, click FTP Locations. Double-click a FTP site, then double-click where you want to save to*

* *To save to a Web server, click Web Folders. Activate a Web folder*

2 Name the workbook   **3** Click here

Interactive saving

You can also use the procedures described here to save

workbook components e.g.:

• single worksheets

• a chart

• a cell range

non-interactively.

Follow steps 1-10, as appropriate, but in step 5 ensure that Add interactivity is not ticked.

On page 63, we looked at how to save data non-interactively. This method produces HTML files which can be viewed in more or less any browser, without the need to have access to Excel 2000. If all you want is to have your data viewed, then this is what you need.

However, you can also publish Excel 2000 worksheets *interactively* to the Internet or Intranets. This technique allows users to interact with your data.

Publishing interactive worksheets

Pull down the File menu and do the following:

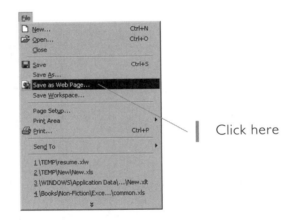

Click here

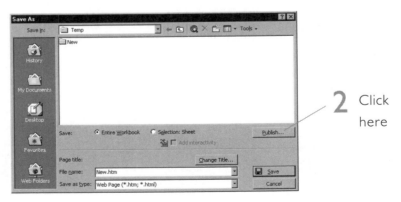

2 Click here

You can't publish the whole of a workbook interactively, only an individual worksheet (or an item on it — see step 4).

Now carry out the following additional steps:

3 Click here; in the list, select the type of data you want to publish

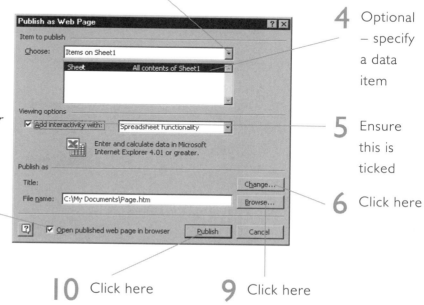

4 Optional – specify a data item

5 Ensure this is ticked

6 Click here

To preview your Web page in your browser, select 'Open published web page in browser' before you carry out step 10.

10 Click here   9 Click here

Re step 9 – complete the Browse dialog which launches, in line with the procedures described in 'Publishing workbooks non-interactively' on page 63.
Finally, perform step 10.

7 Name the published data

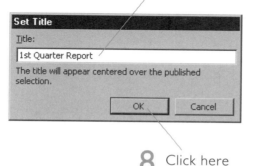

8 Click here

Other save operations

Additional formats you can save to include the following:

- *earlier versions of Excel*
- *various Microsoft Works formats*

Saving to other formats

Excel 2000 lets you save your workbooks to a variety of third-party formats. To do this, refer to page 57, then do the following:

Step 1   Don't select Microsoft Excel Workbook (*.xls); instead, click the relevant external format

Steps 2-5   Perform as normal

Using AutoSave

You can have Excel 2000 save workbooks automatically, at intervals you specify. This is a two-stage process.

Add-Ins are separate programs which add optional features to Excel 2000. AutoSave is installed automatically, but you have to 'load' it in order to use it.

If you haven't used AutoSave before, pull down the Tools menu and click Add-Ins. Do the following:

1 | Click Autosave Add-in

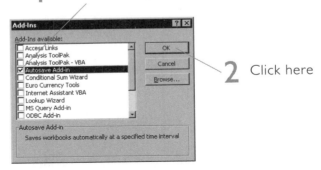

2 Click here

To unload AutoSave (this may improve Excel 2000's performance), repeat steps 1-2.

With AutoSave loaded, pull down the Tools menu and click AutoSave. Do the following:

3 Type in an AutoSave interval

If you want Excel to ask permission before saving your work, ensure this is selected:

4 Click here

Opening workbooks

Re step 4 – if you store workbooks in one folder, you can have the Open dialog default to it.

Pull down the Tools menu and click Options. In the Options dialog, activate the General tab. In the Default file location: field, type in the default folder. Finally, click OK.

When a new workbook has been saved, carry out the following procedure to open it.

Pull down the File menu and click Open. Now carry out the following steps:

3 Click here. In the drop-down list, select the relevant drive

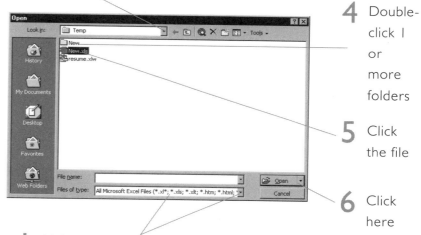

4 Double-click 1 or more folders

5 Click the file

6 Click here

You can copy, rename or delete workbooks from within the Open dialog.

Right-click any workbook entry in the main part of the dialog. In the menu, click the desired option. Now carry out the appropriate action.

An example: to rename a workbook, click Rename in the menu. Type in the new name and press Enter.

1 Make sure 'Microsoft Excel Files...' is shown. If it isn't, click the arrow and follow step 2

```
All Files (*.*)
All Microsoft Excel Files (*.xl*; *.xls; *.xlt; *.htm; *.html; *
Microsoft Excel Files (*.xl*; *.xls; *.xla; *.xlt; *.xlm; *.xlc;
Web Pages (*.htm; *.html)
Text Files (*.prn; *.txt; *.csv)
Query Files (*.iqy; *.dqy; *.oqy; *.rqy)
```

2 Click here

Opening workbooks on the Internet

You can open workbooks stored on:

To open Excel 2000 files on the Web, ensure you have a live Internet connection, then perform steps 1-3.

- any HTTP site on the World Wide Web

- Intranets

Opening a workbook

Pull down the File menu and do the following:

| Click here

Re step 2 – to open an Excel workbook on an Intranet, you might type:

http://server/mine.xls

where 'mine.xls' is the workbook, and 'server' the name of the server.

3 Click here

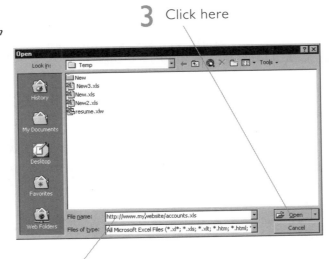

2 Type in the Internet address e.g.:
http://www.mywebsite/accounts.xls

Reopening HTML files

See pages 59-65 for how to generate HTML files from Excel 2000 workbooks/worksheets.

We've already seen that, when you export HTML files in Excel 2000, they can be edited directly from within Internet Explorer 5 (see 'HTML Enhancements' on page 59) with little or no loss of data or formatting. Excel calls this process 'round-tripping'.

The lack of deterioration can be demonstrated further with the help of examples. Study the two illustrations below:

To open a HTML file, follow the procedures on page 67. In steps 1-2, however, select 'Web Pages (*.htm; *.html)'.

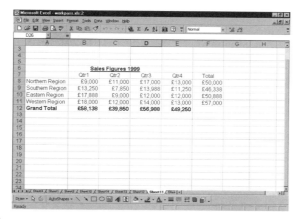

The original workbook...

Here, saving the Excel 2000 workbook to HTML and reopening it has only produced one change: the Zoom setting has been modified slightly.

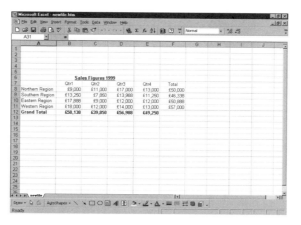

The HTML file after being reopened in Excel 2000

Using workspaces

Sometimes when you work with Excel 2000, you'll require:

- more than one workbook open simultaneously

- multiple worksheets open simultaneously

Instead of having to open each component separately, you can save details of your current working environment as a 'workspace'. When you've done this, you can simply reopen the workspace; Excel 2000 then opens the constituent workbooks/worksheets for you.

Re step 3 – the default file name for a workspace is RESUME.XLW. Change this if you want.

Saving the current environment as a workspace

Pull down the File menu and click Save Workspace. Now carry out the following steps:

Click here. In the drop-down list, select a drive

Repeat step 2 as necessary, until you locate the relevant folder.

3 Optional – name the workspace

4 Click here

To reopen a workspace, follow the procedures on page 67. In steps 1-2, however, click: Workspaces (*.xlw)

2 Double-click the folder where you want to save the workspace

Closing workbooks

There are slightly different procedures in Excel 2000 for closing:

- a single workbook

- multiple workbooks simultaneously

Re step 1 – you can use a keyboard shortcut here instead: simply press Ctrl+W.

Closing one workbook

To close the active workbook, pull down the File menu and do the following:

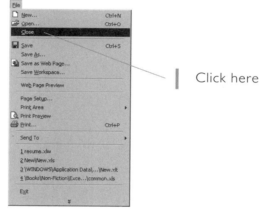

Click here

If the Office Assistant is on-screen when you follow step 1, the warning message looks like this:

![Microsoft Excel - Do you want to save the changes you made to 'New.xls'? Yes No Cancel]

Carry out step 2.

If you've made amendments to the workbook but haven't yet saved them, Excel 2000 now launches a special message. Do the following:

2 Click here to save your work (after the save, Excel closes the workbook)

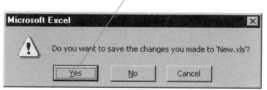

...cont'd

Closing all open workbooks

If several workbooks are currently active, you can close each one singly, if you want. Alternatively, however, you can make use of a shortcut to close them all in one go.

Hold down one Shift key. Pull down the File menu and do the following:

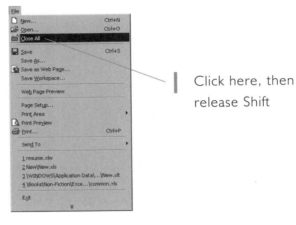

1 Click here, then release Shift

Re step 2 – if other open workbooks have unsaved amendments, Excel launches additional versions of this message; complete them as appropriate.

If you've made amendments to any of the workbooks but haven't yet saved them, Excel 2000 launches a special message. Carry out either step 2 OR 3 below, as appropriate:

If the Office Assistant is on-screen when you follow step 1, the warning message looks like this:

Carry out step 2 OR 3.

2 Click here to save your work in (then close) the first workbook

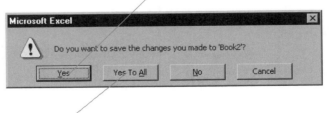

3 Click here to save your work in (then close) *all* open workbooks

Cell referencing

In this chapter, you'll learn how to define cell references. You'll apply relative and absolute references, then discover how to use an older but easier-to-use system: R1C1 referencing. Next, you'll apply names to cells (a technique which makes cell manipulation much more convenient) and delete existing names. Finally, you'll have Excel replace references in formulas with their equivalent names, and paste names into formulas via the Formula Bar.

Covers

Chapter Five

Relative references

Excel 2000 lets you define cell references in various ways. Look at the next illustration:

	A	B	C	D	E
1					
2		Product	Unit Price	Quantity	Amount due
3		Widgets	£0.07	425	£29.75
4		Nuts	£0.13	246	
5		Bolts	£0.08	380	

The following formula has been inserted in cell E3:

C3*D3

This tells Excel to multiply the contents of C3 by D3. C3 and D3 are defined in relation to E3: C3 is in the same row (3) but two columns to the left (C), while D3 is in the same row but *one* column to the left. Excel calls this 'relative referencing'.

That these are relative references can be shown in the following way. If we use the techniques discussed on page 36 (AutoFill) to extend the formula in E3 to E4 and E5, this is the result:

The formulas in E3:E5 have been made visible by pressing Ctrl+'. (To type ' press the key directly beneath the Esc key.)
To hide the formulas again, repeat this.

	C	D	E
1			
2	Unit Price	Quantity	Amount due
3	0.07	425	=C3*D3
4	0.13	246	=C4*D4
5	0.08	380	=C5*D5

Extrapolated cell references

Excel 2000 has extrapolated the references intelligently, correctly divining that the formula in E4 should be C4*D4, and that in E5 C5*D5.

Compare this process with the use of absolute (i.e. unchanging) references on page 75.

Absolute references

We've seen – on page 74 – how useful relative cell references can be. However, there are situations when you need to refer to one or more cells in a way which *doesn't* vary according to circumstances.

Look at the next illustration:

	A	B	C	D	E	F
1	VAT rate=	17.50%				
2		Product	Unit Price	Quantity	Amount due	VAT
3		Widgets	£0.07	425	£29.75	£5.21
4		Nuts	£0.13	246	£31.98	
5		Bolts	£0.08	380	£30.40	

The reason the VAT rate is entered separately from the calculation is convenience: if the rate changes, it's much easier to update one entry, rather than several.

Cell F3 contains a formula which multiplies E3 by B1. If this were inserted as:

=E3*B1

extrapolating the formula over F4 and F5 (with the technique we used on page 74) would produce:

=E4*B2

and

=E5*B3

respectively.

You can also use mixed cell references – i.e. combinations of relative and absolute references.

Clearly, this is incorrect (in this instance) because the cell in which the VAT rate is entered doesn't vary. It's an absolute reference, and remains B1.

Entering absolute references

Entering an absolute reference is easy. Simply insert $ in front of each formula component which won't change.

The correct version of the VAT formula in F3 would therefore be:

=E3*B1

R1C1 referencing

A1 is the referencing method which Excel 2000 uses by default (and which has been used throughout this book).

Excel 2000 can also make use of an older, alternative style of referencing cells (called the 'R1C1' method) by which both columns and rows are numbered. It has the advantage that the distinction between absolute and relative referencing is easier to understand. Its disadvantage is that it is not as brief as the A1 method.

Relative and absolute R1C1 referencing

In R1C1 style, Excel 2000 indicates absolute references as per the following example:

R2C2   the equivalent of B2 in A1 style

In other words, cell location is defined with an 'R' followed by a row number and a 'C' followed by a column number.

On the other hand, R1C1 relative references are enclosed in square brackets. Thus, if the active cell is B5, the relative cell reference R[1]C[1] refers to the cell one row down and one column to the right (i.e. C6).

Implementing R1C1 referencing

Pull down the Tools menu and click Options. Now do the following:

Activate the General tab

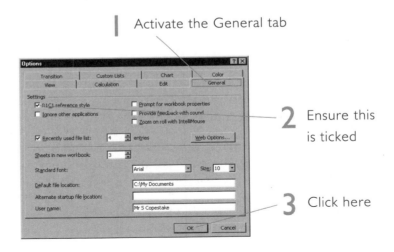

2   Ensure this is ticked

3   Click here

Naming cells

An alternative way to reference cells is to give them a 'name' or identifier which describes the contents. Naming cells is a much more user-friendly technique than working with cell coordinates.

Defining names with the Name box

The easiest way to define names for cells is to use the Name box on the Formula Bar. Select the cell(s) you want to name, then do the following:

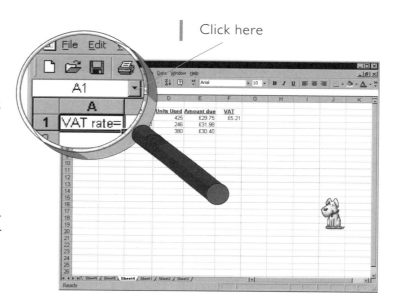

Click here

- The first character must be a letter or underscore
- Other characters may be any sequence of letters, digits, underscores and full stops (but not spaces)
- Separators (as in the example on the right) must be either an underscore or full stop

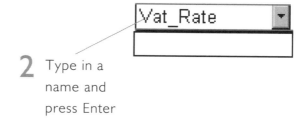

2 Type in a name and press Enter

The Name box is an effective shortcut to applying and inserting names. However, you can also use a more comprehensive menu route to:

- define and apply new names

- apply existing names

- delete names

- substitute already defined names for cell references, either in selected cells or globally

- paste names into the Formula Bar

Defining/applying names – the menu route
Do the following:

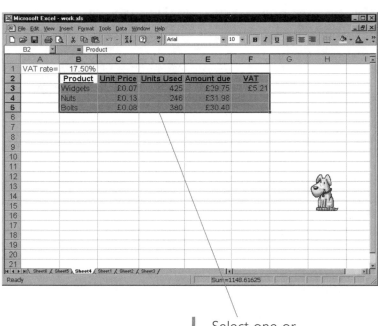

Select one or more cells

2 Pull down the Insert menu and carry out the following additional steps:

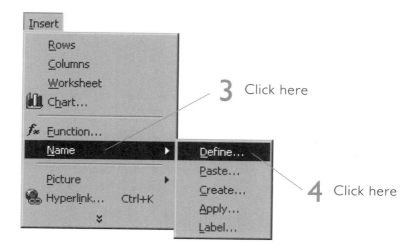

3 Click here

4 Click here

Now carry out step 5 OR 6 below. Finally, perform step 7:

5 Type in a new name

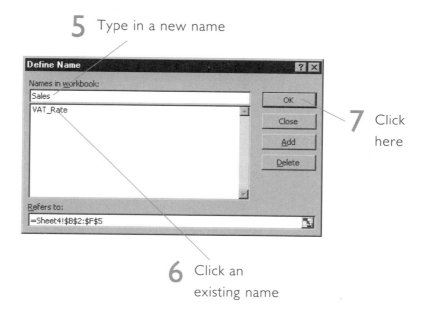

7 Click here

6 Click an existing name

Deleting names

Deleting names
Pull down the Insert menu and carry out the following steps:

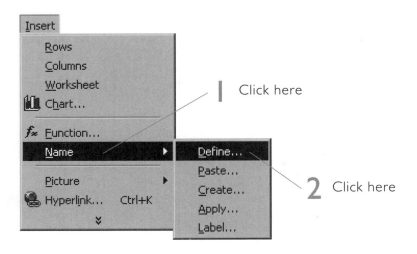

1 Click here

2 Click here

5 Click here

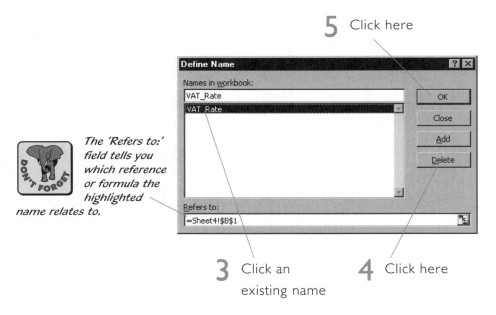

The 'Refers to:' field tells you which reference or formula the highlighted name relates to.

3 Click an existing name

4 Click here

Substituting names in formulas

You can have Excel 2000 automatically replace normal cell references in formulas with the appropriate pre-defined names.

The illustration below should clarify the need for this:

	A	B	C	D	E	F	G	H
1	VAT rate=	17.50%						
2		**Product**	**Unit Price**	**Units Used**	**Amount due**	**VAT**		
3		Widgets	£0.07	425	£29.75	£5.21		
4		Nuts	£0.13	246	£31.98			
5		Bolts	£0.08	380	£30.40			
6								
7								
8								
9								
10								
11								
12		**Total amount due =**	£92.13					
13								
14								
15								
16								
17								

Sheet5 / Sheet6 / **Sheet4** / Sheet1 / Sheet2 / Sheet3

The example shown here is a particularly simple one; name substitution comes into its own in large worksheets.

C12 contains this formula:

=SUM(E3:E5)

which totals E3, E4 and E5. If, however, these cells have had names allocated to them (e.g. 'Widget_total', 'Nut_total' and 'Bolt_total'), then it makes sense to adjust the formula in C12 accordingly. Fortunately, you can have Excel 2000 do this for you.

If you want to limit the swap to a single cell, select it and one other which contains no formulas.

Substituting names for references

Do ONE of the following:

1. Select the cells which contain the formulas whose references you want converted to the relevant names

2. Click any one cell in the worksheet if you want *all* formula references converted to the relevant names

Now carry out the additional procedures on page 82.

Now pull down the Insert menu and click Name, Apply. Carry out the following additional steps:

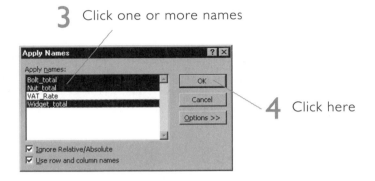

3 Click one or more names

4 Click here

The end result:

Excel 2000 has inserted the relevant names into the formula

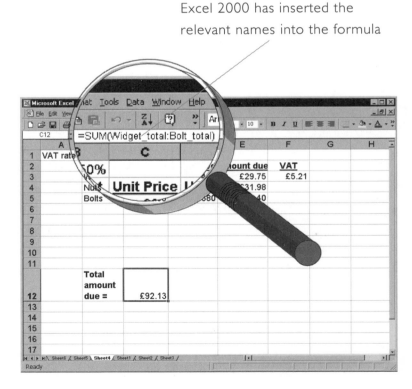

Pasting names

Excel 2000 lets you paste names directly into the Formula Bar while you're in the process of entering a formula.

Select the cell into which you want to insert the formula. Activate the Formula Bar by clicking in it. Begin the formula by typing:

=

Now pull down the Insert menu and do the following:

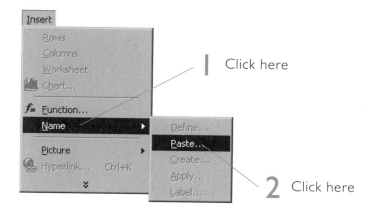

| Click here

2 Click here

3 Click a name

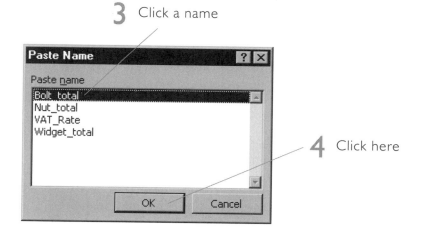

4 Click here

Cell reference operators

We've already encountered one cell reference operator: the colon. This is known as the Range operator and is used to define the rectangular block of cells formed between the two cell references which it separates. For example, A5:E7 defines the block of cells which begins with A5 and ends with E7.

However, there are two other reference operators. Look at the next illustration:

With Intersection operators, the defining ranges must overlap. If they don't, Excel 2000 returns this error message:

	A	B	C	D	E
1					
2		Qtr1	Qtr2	Qtr3	Qtr4
3	1997	£8,000	£10,000	£15,000	£12,000
4	1998	£9,000	£11,000	£17,000	£13,000
5	1999	£10,000	£12,000	£19,000	£14,000
6					
7	Quarter 3 sales for 1997-1999=				£51,000
8	Quarter 3 sales for 1998				£17,000

E7 contains this formula:

=SUM(D3,D4,D5)

The selections in the illustration below show where B4:E4 and D3:D5 (see the example on the right) intersect:

The comma is known as the Union operator; it combines multiple references into one. In this case, the formula is totalling separate cells which could also be expressed as: D3:D5. However, this need not be the case. For instance, it could show: A3,B5,E8...

E8 contains the following formula:

=SUM(B4:E4 D3:D5)

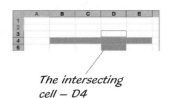

The intersecting cell – D4

The space separating the two ranges is known as the Intersection operator. The formula returns the cell at the intersection of B4:E4 and D3:D5 – in other words, D4.

Functions

In this chapter, you'll learn how to insert functions into your formulas. Excel 2000 has a very large number of inbuilt functions which perform specialised calculations for wide-ranging applications e.g. statistical, mathematical, financial, etc. You'll learn how to utilise some of the most frequently used functions (including HYPERLINK, which inserts links to other worksheets/documents, even those on Intranets or the Internet).

You'll also discover how to use the simpler functions on-the-fly, by reference to Excel 2000's Status bar.

Covers

Chapter Six

Functions – an overview

Functions are pre-defined tools which accomplish specific tasks. These tasks are often calculations; occasionally, however, they're more generalised (e.g. some functions simply return dates and/or times). In effect, functions replace one or more formulas.

Excel provides a special dialog – the Formula Palette – to help ensure that you enter functions correctly. This is useful for the following reasons:

- Excel 2000 provides so many functions, it's very convenient to apply (and amend) them from a centralised source

- the Formula Palette ensures the functions are entered with the correct syntax

Functions can only be used in formulas, and are always followed by bracketed arguments.

Recognising functions

The following are examples of often-used functions:

Sum=£92.13

SUM	Adds together a range of numbers
AVERAGE	Finds the average of a range of numbers
MAX	Finds the largest number in a range
MIN	Finds the smallest number in a range
LOOKUP	Compares a specified value with a specified cell range and returns a value
IF	Verifies if a condition is true or false, and acts accordingly

None
Average
Count
Count Nums
Max
Min
✓ Sum

Click a function

Some of the above are explored later in the chapter.

Inserting a function

You can also use another route to insert a function. Do the following.

Click in a cell. Pull down the Insert menu and click Function. In the Function category: field in the Paste Function dialog, select a heading. Click a function in the Function name: box. Click OK.

Excel now launches the Formula Palette – complete steps 4 and 5.

Inserting a function with the Formula Palette

At the relevant juncture during the process of inserting a formula, refer to the Formula Bar and do the following:

Click here

Now carry out the following steps:

2 Click here

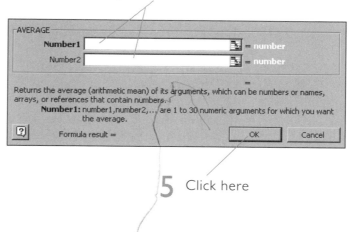

3 Select a function

To edit an existing function, click the relevant cell. Click this button:

4 Enter the function arguments

in the Formula Bar. The Formula Palette launches, with the existing function displayed in the Formula Bar. Amend this and/or its arguments in the Palette. Finally, click OK.

5 Click here

The SUM function

If you haven't used it recently, the AutoSum button may be on the toolbar flyout – click:

to launch it.

The SUM function totals specified cells. You can insert a SUM function by using the Formula Palette – see page 87. However, you can also use a useful shortcut – AutoSum – to total adjacent cells automatically. Look at the next illustration:

	A	B	C	D	E	F
1						
2		Qtr1	Qtr2	Qtr3	Qtr4	Totals
3	1997	£8,000	£10,000	£15,000	£12,000	
4	1998	£9,000	£11,000	£17,000	£13,000	
5	1999	£10,000	£12,000	£19,000	£14,000	

You can use a shortcut here. Pre-select the cells you want to total before you carry out step 1. For instance, if you select B3:F6 and then click the AutoSum button, Excel 2000 inserts all relevant totals:

To total the range B3:E3 in F3, click cell F3. Now refer to the Standard toolbar and do the following:

Click the AutoSum button

Excel 2000 surrounds the cells it believes should be included in the SUM function with a dotted line:

	A	B	C	D	E	F
1						
2		Qtr1	Qtr2	Qtr3	Qtr4	Totals
3	1997	£8,000	£10,000	£15,000	£12,000	=SUM(A3:E3)
4	1998	£9,000	£11,000	£17,000	£13,000	
5	1999	£10,000	£12,000	£19,000	£14,000	
6	Totals					

Amend the formula entry in F3, if necessary (in this instance, change A3:E3 to B3:E3). Then press Enter; Excel 2000 inserts the SUM function.

The LOOKUP function

LOOKUP compares a value you set (the Look-Up value) with the first row or column in a Look-Up table. If it finds a matching value, it returns it in the cell you specify. If it doesn't, it returns the largest value in the table which is the same as or less than the Look-Up value

LOOKUP can also work with text values and/or names.

Alternatively, if the Look-Up value is smaller than all the values in the Look-Up table, LOOKUP returns the following error:

#N/A

The values in the Look-Up table must be in ascending order. If they're not, you can rectify this. Select the values. Pull down the Data menu and click Sort. If the Sort Warning dialog appears, make the relevant choice and click Sort. In the Sort by section in the Sort dialog, make sure Ascending is selected. Finally, click OK.

(For more information on sorting, see page 125.)

Study the next illustration:

The Look-Up value

	A	B	C	D	E	F
1						
2						
3	Monthly lease rates per £1000 borrowed					
4	**Years**	**Rates**				
5	1	£22.50				
6	2	£26.58				
7	3	£47.31				
8	4	£49.22		Lease term in years=		50
9	5	£89.08		Lease value=		

The Look-Up table

Here, a Look-Up table and value have been established. In this instance, names have also been applied, for convenience:

- the table (B5:B9) is Lease_Table

- the value (F8) is Lease_Term

It only remains to enter and define the LOOKUP function – see page 90 for how to do this.

Using LOOKUP

Select the relevant cell (in the example on page 89, F9). Follow steps 1-2 on page 87. Now carry out the following additional steps:

If you've used it before, LOOKUP may well be in the main body of the menu, instead: — *If so, simply click it (and omit steps 3-5).*

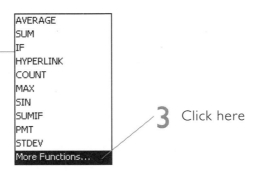

3 Click here

4 Click here

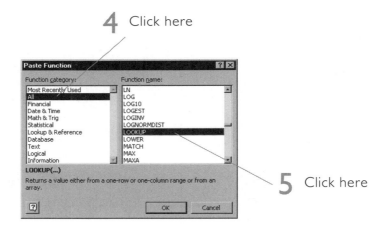

5 Click here

6 Click here

7 Click here

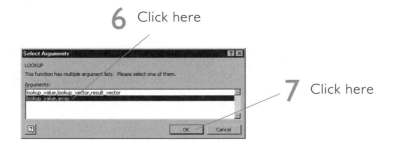

Re steps 8 and 9 – in this example, names have been entered since they've been applied to the relevant cells.

Now carry out the following additional steps:

8 Type in the Look-Up value reference

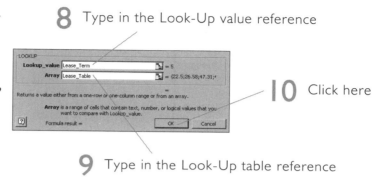

10 Click here

9 Type in the Look-Up table reference

The end result:

The inserted formula

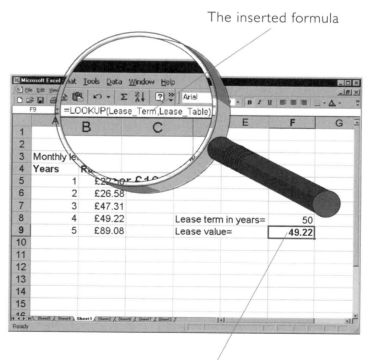

The final result: in this instance, LOOKUP has returned the highest value under 50

The IF function

The IF function checks whether a specified condition is TRUE or FALSE and carries out one or more specified actions accordingly.

Look at the next illustration:

	A	B	C	D
1				
2				
3		**Name**	**Amount Spent**	**Discount**
4				
5		Brierley	1,280	
6		Jones	1,020	
7		Mitchell	570	
8		Harrison	1150	
9		Wood	870	

Here, Individual customer discounts need to be calculated in D5:D9. Each discount in D5:D9 depends on the following conditions:

- if the amount a customer has spent is greater than or equal to £1000, then the discount is 20%

- if the amount a customer has spent is less than £1000 then the discount is 10%

Using the IF Function

Re step 1 – if IF isn't listed, click More Functions instead. In the Function category: field in the Paste Function dialog, click Logical. In the Function name: box, select IF. Click OK.

First, select the cell you want to host the function – in the case of the example above, D5 (initially). Follow steps 1-2 on page 87. Now carry out step 3 below:

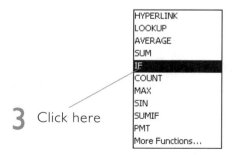

3 Click here

Perform the remaining steps on page 93.

...cont'd

Carry out the following additional steps:

4 Enter the 'logical test'

See the Glossary below for an explanation of the terms used in steps 4-6.

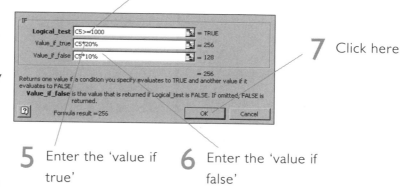

IF		
Logical_test	C5>=1000	= TRUE
Value_if_true	C5*20%	= 256
Value_if_false	C5*10%	= 128

= 256

Returns one value if a condition you specify evaluates to TRUE and another value if it evaluates to FALSE.

Value_if_false is the value that is returned if Logical_test is FALSE. If omitted, FALSE is returned.

Formula result = 256   [OK] [Cancel]

7 Click here

5 Enter the 'value if true'

6 Enter the 'value if false'

The IF function uses comparison operators – see page 43 for details.

Glossary

Logical test	The condition. In this instance: C5>=1000 (i.e. the contents of C5 must be greater than or equal to 1000)
Value if true	The action to be taken if the condition is met. In this instance: C5*20% (i.e. the contents of C5 are multiplied by 20%)
Value if false	The action to be taken if the condition isn't met. In this instance: C5*10% (i.e. the contents of C5 are multiplied by 10%)

To activate a hyperlink (they appear in blue and are underlined – see page 94 for more information), do the following:

Click to see report

Click here

The end result:

Name	Amount Spent	Discount
Brierley	1,280	256
Jones	1,020	204
Mitchell	570	57
Harrison	1150	230
Wood	870	87

The IF function has been inserted into D5, and extrapolated into D6:D9 with AutoFill

The HYPERLINK function

Re step 4 – to include specific cells in the link, carry out the following:

• *surround the address details in square brackets*

• *add the range reference later*

For example, to link to cells B3:C6 in the worksheet 'Annual' in the workbook 'Accounts.xls' stored at 'www.commerce.com', type (without line breaks or spaces):

[http://www.commerce. com/accounts.xls] Annual!B3:C6

You can use the HYPERLINK function to insert links to documents on:

• network servers

• Intranets/the Internet

• local hard disks

Hyperlinks can also include pointers to:

• specific cells or ranges in Excel 2000 worksheets

• Word 2000 bookmarks

Using the HYPERLINK function

First, select the cell you want to host the function. Follow steps 1-2 on page 87. Now do the following:

3 Click here

Re step 4 – to link to a Word 2000 bookmark, type the bookmark name immediately after the bracketed address e.g.:

[c:\mywork\report.doc] bookmark

(Include no line breaks or spaces.)

4 Enter link details

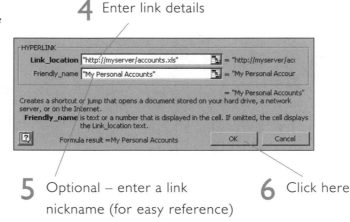

5 Optional – enter a link nickname (for easy reference)

6 Click here

Cell errors and auditing

This chapter provides details of common error messages which arise when Excel 2000 is unable to evaluate a formula. These are shown 'on-the-fly', with reference to specific examples and also with the appropriate corrections. Excel 2000 supplies a set of auditing tools to help trace errors; you'll learn how to use these to track dependent and precedent cells. You'll also use the Error Tracer to pinpoint cells which are in conflict with formulas.

Finally, you'll insert comments into cells, and edit or delete them subsequently.

Covers

Chapter Seven

Cell errors

The following table shows details of some of the common Excel 2000 error messages (they're shown in action in the illustration below).

#DIV/0!   In this instance, this error is caused by an attempt to divide 2.5 by zero. Theoretically this should generate infinity. In practice any such value is too big, even for a computer, and the calculation is suppressed

#N/A   This means that No value is Available. The LOOKUP argument (B8, B5:D6) should refer to cell D8 instead of B8; B8 – since it contains text – is incorrect

#NAME?   Excel 2000 fails to recognise the Name of the function 'IS', which has been incorrectly typed for 'IF'

#NULL!   This formula uses the intersection operator (a space) to locate the cell at the intersection of ranges B15:D15 and A16:A18. Since they don't intersect, Excel 2000 displays the error message

The data/ error messages are on the left of the illustration; the formulas which gave rise to the errors are on the right.

	A	B	C	D		D
1	(1)					
2		2.5	0	#DIV/0!		=B2/C2
3						
4	(2)					
5	Amount:	£0	£500	£1,000		1000
6	Discount:	0.0%	5.0%	10.0%		0.1
7						
8		Price =		£750		750
9		Discount Rate =		#N/A		=LOOKUP(B8, B5:D6)
10						
11	(3)					
12		-0.25		#NAME?		=IS(B12=0, "Zero", "Non-zero")
13						
14	(4)					
15		5	10	15		15
16	2					
17	4					
18	6			#NULL!		=B15:D15 A16:A18

The above error messages in action

Here are some additional error messages, and details of their causes:

#NUM!   This error value indicates problems with numbers. The first example of this error (see below) attempts to generate the value 100^{1000}, i.e. 100 multiplied by itself 1000 times. This is too large for the computer to store and so the calculation is suppressed

In the second example the attempt to calculate the square root (SQRT function) of a negative value is suppressed

#VALUE!   This error occurs when the data in a cell isn't appropriate for the operation, or the operation doesn't apply to the type of data. Here an attempt has been made to divide 'Text' by 50

This error is not necessarily generated by a formula. In this case the number stored is simply too long for the cell width

The number of hash symbols – # – varies according to the column size.

The data/ error messages are on the left of the illustration; the formulas which gave rise to the errors are on the right.

	A	B	C	D		D
20	(5)					
21		100	1000	#NUM!		=B21^C21
22		16		#NUM!		=SQRT(-B22)
23						
24	(6)					
25		Text	50	#VALUE!		=B25/C25
26						
27	(7)					
28				########		100000000
29						
30	(8)					
31		100				
32			50	2		=B31/C32

The examples on pages 96-98 are simple, practical illustrations of the causes of error messages. In practice, tracking down the origin of an error message is sometimes less than straightforward, because a single error may cause a proliferation of error values.
(See pages 99-101 for tracking techniques.)

The final error message we'll discuss here is slightly more complex:

#REF!   To generate this error requires another stage. On page 97, the formula in D32 (=B31/C32) divides the contents of cell B31 by the contents of cell C32, initially producing the correct answer. However, if Excel 2000 can't locate one of the cells referred to (for instance, if B31 no longer exists because row 31 has been deleted), it displays this message

This process is demonstrated in the illustration below:

#REF! only appears if you've deleted the cell referred to by a formula; clearing the cell's contents (e.g. by selecting it and clicking Clear, Contents in the Edit menu) will, instead, produce '0'.

2 The formula has changed; the B31 component has been replaced by #REF! and C32 has now become C31

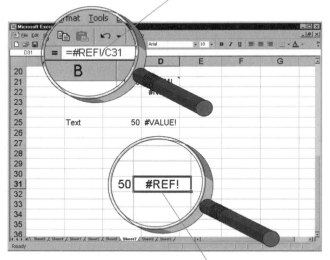

Since row 31 has been deleted and the reference in the formula to B31 is invalid, Excel 2000 displays the error message

Auditing tools

Excel 2000 provides a variety of features you can use to ensure formulas work correctly. You can use the Auditing toolbar to have Excel delineate cell relationships with arrows ('tracers'). In this way, if a formula returns an error message, you can track down which cell is misbehaving.

Cells which are referred to by a formula in another cell are called precedents. For example, if cell H26 has the formula:

=M97

M97 is a precedent.

Inserting precedent tracers

Click the cell whose precedents you want to display. Pull down the Tools menu and click Auditing, Show Auditing Toolbar. Now do the following:

Click here

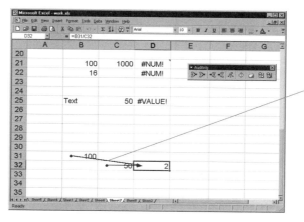

Precedent tracers – D32 (selected) hosts a formula whose precedents are B31 and C32

Cells which contain formulas referring to other cells are called dependents. For instance, if cell H6 has the formula:

=SUM(C6:D8)

H6 is a dependent cell (and the cells in the range C6:D8 are precedent cells – see page 99).

Inserting dependent tracers

Select a cell which is referred to in a formula. Pull down the Tools menu and click Auditing, Show Auditing Toolbar. Now do the following:

To remove all tracer arrows on the worksheet (e.g. when you've finished the audit, or perhaps to start again from a different cell), simply click this button:

in the Auditing toolbar.

Click here

Before carrying out the procedures here, pull down the Tools menu and click Options. Activate the View tab; in the Objects section, ensure Show all is selected. Finally, click OK.

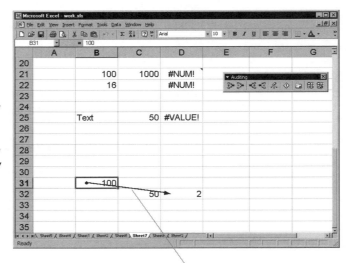

A dependent tracer – B31 (selected) is referenced by the formula in D32, and the tracer highlights this

Using the Error Tracer

When a formula returns an error, you can use another auditing tool – the Error Tracer – to track it back to its source and then correct it.

Using the Error Tracer

Select a cell which contains an error value. Pull down the Tools menu and click Auditing, Show Auditing Toolbar. Now do the following:

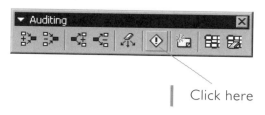

Click here

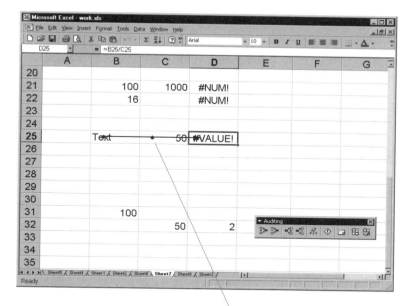

Excel 2000 flags all cells referred to by the incorrect formula in D25

Working with comments

Red comment flag

You can attach comments to cells. Once inserted, comments can be viewed or edited at will.

1.   Inserting a comment

Select the relevant cell. Pull down the Insert menu and click Comment. Now do the following:

If the Comment flag doesn't appear, pull down the Tools menu and click Options. Activate the View tab. Select Comment indicator only. Click OK.

Comment box

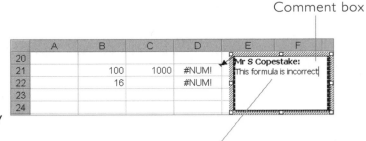

Type in the comment, then click outside the box

2.   Editing a comment

Select the relevant cell (for how to recognise cells which contain comments, see the upper DON'T FORGET tip). Pull down the Insert menu and click Edit Comment. Now click inside the Comment box and amend the text as necessary. Click outside the box when you've finished.

To have all comments (and flags) display all the time, pull down the Tools menu and click Options. Activate the View tab. Select Comment & indicator. Click OK.
   (If you do this, don't pull down the Insert menu in procedures 2. and 3. – the comment already displays.)

3.   Deleting a comment

Click any cell which contains a comment. Pull down the Insert menu and click Edit Comment. Now do the following:

Click the Comment box frame, then press Delete

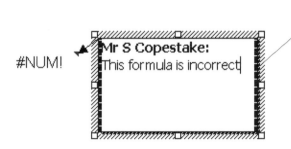

Workbook security

In this chapter, you'll restrict access to your workbooks by allocating passwords, then reopen them. You'll also prevent unauthorised users from modifying the structure of constituent worksheets and resizing workbook windows. Finally, you'll 'protect' worksheets, a technique which allows you to specify precisely which cells can and can't be amended.

Covers

Chapter Eight

Protecting workbooks

You can protect your workbooks by:

- allocating an 'Open' password

- allocating a 'Modify' password

The first allows users to open the associated workbook but prevents them from saving changes *under the existing filename*. The second, on the other hand, allows users to modify and save the workbook.

If you lose or forget the password, you won't be able to recover the workbook!

Passwords are case-sensitive, and can be up to 15 characters long. They can be any combination of letters, numbers, spaces and other symbols.

You impose passwords in the course of carrying out a Save As operation.

Allocating a password

Pull down the File menu and click Save As. Now carry out steps 1-5 below:

*Re step 2 – click any buttons here: for access to the relevant folders. (For instance, to save files to your Desktop, click Desktop.)
Ignore step 3.*

2 Click here. In the drop-down list, click a drive

5 Click here

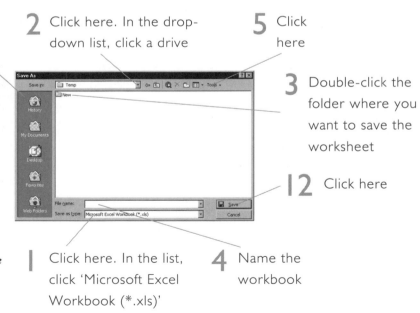

3 Double-click the folder where you want to save the worksheet

2 Click here

Repeat step 3 as necessary, until you locate the relevant folder.

1 Click here. In the list, click 'Microsoft Excel Workbook (*.xls)'

4 Name the workbook

After step 5, perform the additional steps on page 105.

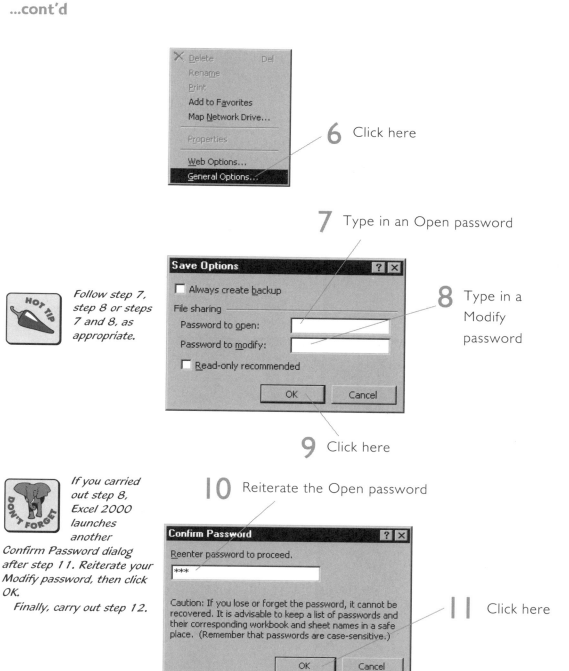

6 Click here

7 Type in an Open password

Follow step 7, step 8 or steps 7 and 8, as appropriate.

8 Type in a Modify password

9 Click here

10 Reiterate the Open password

If you carried out step 8, Excel 2000 launches another Confirm Password dialog after step 11. Reiterate your Modify password, then click OK.

Finally, carry out step 12.

11 Click here

Finally, carry out step 12 on page 104.

Opening protected workbooks

Once passwords have been allocated to a file, you can modify or remove them.

With the file open, pull down the File menu and click Save As. Carry out steps 1-6 on pages 104-105. Now do the following:

Opening a password-protected workbook

Pull down the File menu and do the following:

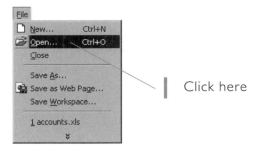

1 Click here

A Retype or delete the password(s)

B Click here

Excel 2000 launches the Confirm Password dialog; complete this as per steps 10-11 on page 105. If you altered/deleted both passwords, complete the further dialog which launches.

Finally, carry out step 12 on page 104.

4 Click here. In the drop-down list, select the relevant drive

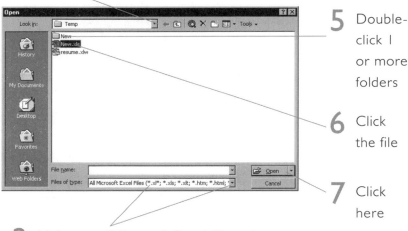

5 Double-click 1 or more folders

6 Click the file

7 Click here

2 Make sure 'Microsoft Excel Files...' is shown. If it isn't, click the arrow and follow step 3

3 Click here

Now carry out steps 8-9 if you allocated an open password:

If you enter the wrong Open or Modify password, Excel 2000 launches a message. Do the following:

Click here

Now repeat the relevant procedures on pages 106-107. When you re-enter the password(s), however, ensure that:

- *the Caps Lock key is not active*

- *you type in the password with the correct capitalisation (passwords are case-sensitive)*

8 Type in the Open password

9 Click here

If the workbook you're opening has had a modify passwords allocated to it, Excel launches a further dialog. Carry out steps 10 and 11 below to open the workbook with the ability to modify it and save changes under the original name. Alternatively, carry out step 12 alone to open the workbook as a 'read-only' file (i.e. any amendments you make subsequently must be saved under a different name).

10 Type in the modify password

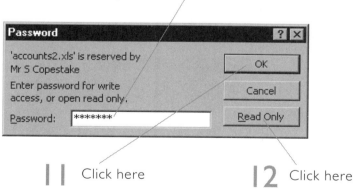

11 Click here

12 Click here

Protecting workbook structure

You can 'protect' the following workbook aspects:

- structure (this prevents worksheets from being deleted, renamed, moved or inserted)

- windows (this prevents workbook windows from being resized, moved or closed)

When the above are active, the relevant menu commands are greyed out.

Protecting a workbook
Pull down the Tools menu and do the following:

To remove protection from the active workbook, pull down the Tools menu and click Protection, Unprotect Workbook.

If you want to apply a password to the workbook (to prevent other users from disabling protection), type in a password in the Password field, then carry out step 4. Now do the following:

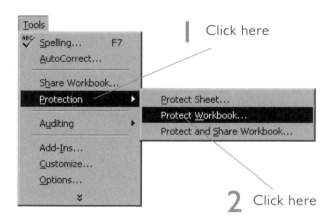

Click here

2 Click here

A Retype your password

B Click here

3 Click either or both of these

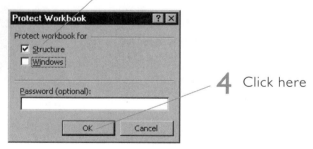

4 Click here

Protecting cells

You can have Excel 2000 warn you when you're about to open a workbook containing macros (small, independent programs – see Chapter 15) which might contain harmful viruses.

Pull down the Tools menu and click Macro, Security. Activate the Security Level tab. Select a protection level and click OK.

Note that Excel can't actually verify whether viruses are present; it can only warn you of the possibility...

Cells can be protected so that their contents are not overwritten. This is a two-stage process:

1. 'Unlocking' those cells which you'll want to amend *after* the host worksheet has been protected (you won't be able to modify any of the other cells)

2. Protecting the worksheet

Unlocking cells

Select the cells you want to unlock. Pull down the Format menu and do the following:

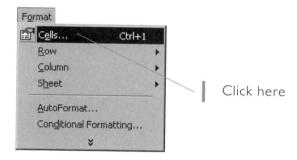

Click here

2 Ensure this tab is activated

If you select this field: the formula(s) in the selected cell(s) will be hidden (provided you've protected the host sheet and selected Contents in the Protect Sheet dialog in step 3 on page 110).

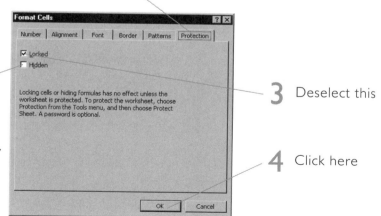

3 Deselect this

4 Click here

...cont'd

If you want to modify cell protection, pull down the Tools menu and click Protection, Unprotect Sheet. If necessary, type in the relevant password in the Unprotect Sheet dialog and click OK. Then select the relevant cells. Press Ctrl+1. Activate the Protection tab in the Format Cells dialog; select or deselect Locked, as appropriate. Click OK.

Finally, perform steps 1-3 again.

Protecting the host worksheet

Pull down the Format menu and do the following:

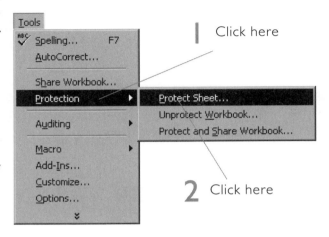

Click here

2 Click here

3 In the Protect Sheet dialog, set 1 or more protection levels. If necessary, type in a password. Finally, click OK.

The effects of cell protection

When you've protected cells, the following results apply:

1. Any attempt to overwrite/edit a locked cell produces a special message:

If the Office Assistant is on-screen, this message becomes:

2. When a locked cell is selected, certain menu commands are greyed out

3. If a locked cell is selected, pressing Tab will move the cursor to the next locked cell (the movement is from top to bottom, and left to right). Pressing Shift+Tab reverses the direction

Data analysis

In this chapter, you'll explore how to preview changes to selected data values and gauge the effect on the overall data pattern, and how to extrapolate predictions based on current figures and formulas. You'll also switch to manual (rather than automatic) calculation, a useful technique in especially large worksheets, and apply PivotTables and PivotCharts to reformulate data dynamically.

Covers

Chapter Nine

Data analysis – an overview

Look at the following worksheet extract:

Note that this excerpt contains the following formulas:

Cell D6   D4*D5
Cell D10   D6-D8

Some of the examples later in this chapter will make use of these.

	A	B	C	D
1				
2		**Video Rentals**		
3				
4		Rental Price=		£2.00
5		Number of Rentals=		250
6		Total Income=		£500
7				
8		Total Costs=		£200
9				
10		Net Profit=		£300
11				

By default, Excel 2000 recalculates formulas in dependent cells when the values in precedent cells are changed. If the network of dependent formulas is large, you may have to wait for the update to finish. This is frustrating if you wish to change several values and have to wait after each one while the rest of the worksheet is recalculated.

To have formulas calculated manually instead, see the margin icons on page 113.

Here, we have a simple worksheet which calculates the Net Profit based on several data values relating to the renting out of videos.

You should bear the following in mind:

Total Income (D6)   = Rental Price (D4) x Number of Rentals (D5)

Net Profit (D10)   = Total Income (D6) – Total Costs (D8)

See the HOT TIP for details of formulas contained in the extract.

Later topics in this chapter will explore various techniques which allow you to interpolate data into the extract conveniently and easily. Once interpolated, changes to data values will ripple through the extract automatically, and can be viewed (and later discarded, if required) at will.

Using Goal Seek

Refer back to the illustration on page 112 and consider the following:

Let's suppose we need to know the number of video rentals necessary to break even. In other words, we want to find out how many rentals are necessary to meet the total costs, thereby ensuring that the net profit is £0. In the case of a simple example like this, you could arrive at the correct figure manually, by trial and error, without too much time and effort. However, more complex worksheets would clearly make this approach impracticable.

Instead, however, you can use a Goal Seek What-If test.

Applying a Goal Seek What-If test

First, select the cell which contains the formula you need to resolve (in this instance, D10). Pull down the Tools menu and do the following:

To turn on manual calculation globally, pull down the Tools menu and click Options. In the Options dialog, activate the Calculation tab. Select Manual in the Calculation section. Finally, click OK.
(For how to activate manual calculation in respect of open worksheets only, see the tips below.)

To invoke manual calculation within all open worksheets, simply press F9.

To invoke manual calculation within the active worksheet only, press Shift+F9.

Click here

Now carry out the following steps:

2 Type in the target value (in this case, 0)

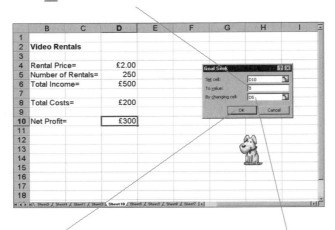

4 Click here

3 Type in the reference of the cell you want to change (in this case, D5)

Excel 2000 has calculated the What-If value...

Re step 5 – click the Cancel button instead if you don't want the result of the Goal Seek inserted permanently into your worksheet.

The ability not to implement the Goal Seek results makes this a useful technique for exploring alternatives.

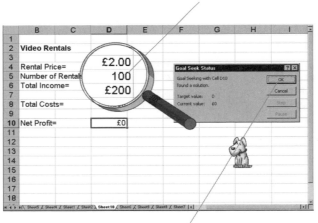

5 Click here to update the worksheet

One-variable data tables

Please refer back to the illustration on page 112 and consider the following additional hypothesis:

Let's suppose we wanted to know how the Net Profit would change when the Rental Price is changed. We could do this using the simple What-If technique of varying the Rental Price and recording the corresponding change in the Net Profit. However, it would be necessary to repeat this for as many separate rental price values as we wished to test.

A much simpler and quicker route is to use a one-variable data table.

Applying a one-variable data table

Carry out the following steps:

Re step 2 – enter the formula which returns the Net Profit. Here, you simply refer to the relevant cell:

=D10

Re step 2 – if you insert values in a column, the formula cell must be in the row above the first value, and one cell to the right. If you type in values in a row, however, it must be in the column to the left of the first value, and one cell below.

One-variable tables will only work if these conditions are met.

2 Type in the necessary formula (but see the tips on the left)

	A	B	C	D	E	F	G	H
1								
2		Video Rentals				Rental Price	Net Profit	
3							£300	
4		Rental Price=		£2.00		£1.00		
5		Number of Rentals=		250		£1.25		
6		Total Income=		£500		£1.50		
7						£1.75		
8		Total Costs=		£200		£2.00		
9						£2.25		
10		Net Profit=		£300		£2.50		
11								
12								
13								
14								
15								
16								
17								
18								
19								

Sheet5 / Sheet4 / Sheet1 / Sheet2 / Sheet10 / Sheet6 / Sheet8 / **Sheet8** / Sheet7 /

1 In a row or column (in this case, F4:F10), type in the values for which you want to generate alternatives

Now select the table. Pull down the Data menu and click Table. Then carry out the following steps:

You must select both columns or rows (but not the headings).

The selected table

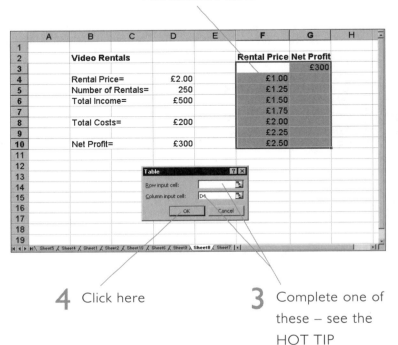

Re step 3 – complete the Column input cell field if you created a columnar table, the Row input cell field if you created a row-based table.

You should enter the reference of the input cell for which the initial table values (in this case, F4:F10) are to be substituted. Here, enter 'D4'.

4 Click here

3 Complete one of these – see the HOT TIP

Rental Price	Net Profit
	£300
£1.00	50
£1.25	112.5
£1.50	175
£1.75	237.5
£2.00	300
£2.25	362.5
£2.50	425

The completed one-variable table

Two-variable data tables

Please refer back to the illustration on page 112 and consider the following:

So far, the examples we've examined have been fairly simple. Suppose, however, that we need to know how the Net Profit would vary relative to *both* of the following:

- the Rental Price

- the Number of Rentals

Excel 2000 has a technique we can use to extrapolate this, too, despite the increased complexity of the operation. We need to use a two-variable data table.

Applying a two-variable data table

Construct the appropriate table – refer to the illustration below as a guide. Then do the following:

Re step 1 – the correct cell reference in this example is F4.

| Select the cell at the intersection of the row containing the first input values and the column containing the second

	D	E	F	G	H	I	J	K
1								
2			Rental			Net Profit		
3			Price			Number of Rentals		
4	£2.00		£300.00	100	125	150	175	200
5	250		£1.00					
6	£500		£1.25					
7			£1.50					
8	£200		£1.75					
9			£2.00					
10	£300		£2.25					
11			£2.50					

Re step 2 – in this example, the input categories are as follows:

- *rental price*

- *number of rentals*

Therefore, the cell which relates to them is D10 (i.e. Net Profit) and the formula is:

=D10

2 Type in the formula which relates to the two input categories

Now select the table. This stage is crucial. The selection must include:

- the formula cell (F4 in the example on page 117)

- the row and column of input data (F5:F11 and G4:K4 in the example on page 117)

- the empty body of the table (G5:K11 in the example on page 117)

Pull down the Data menu and click Table. Now do the following:

Re step 3 – in the current example, the cell which relates to the number of rentals is D5.

3 Type in the reference for the cell which relates to the number of rentals

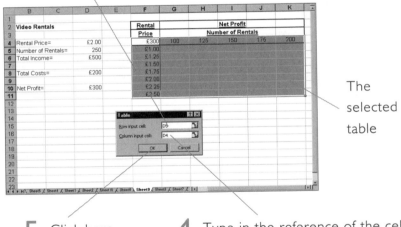

The selected table

Re step 4 – in the current example, the cell which relates to the rental price is D4.

5 Click here

4 Type in the reference of the cell which relates to the rental price

The table shows at a glance the rental price/ number of rentals relationship.

Rental	Net Profit				
Price	Number of Rentals				
£300	100	125	150	175	200
£1.00	-£100.00	-£75.00	-£50.00	-£25.00	£0.00
£1.25	-£75.00	-£43.75	-£12.50	£18.75	£50.00
£1.50	-£50.00	-£12.50	£25.00	£62.50	£100.00
£1.75	-£25.00	£18.75	£62.50	£106.25	£150.00
£2.00	£0.00	£50.00	£100.00	£150.00	£200.00
£2.25	£25.00	£81.25	£137.50	£193.75	£250.00
£2.50	£50.00	£112.50	£175.00	£237.50	£300.00

The completed table

What-If scenarios

Refer back to the illustration on page 112 and consider the following:

Let's suppose we need to forecast the effect of changing the following values:

- the Rental Price (D4)

- the Number of Rentals (D5)

- the Total Cost (D8)

To view a scenario in action, pull down the Tools menu and click Scenarios. In the Scenarios field in the Scenario Manager dialog, highlight a scenario. Click:

Now click:

We could simply input revised values directly into the worksheet and observe the effects. However, if the revisions are simply putative, or if we need to input the same revisions more than once (or in varying combinations), it makes more sense to use a scenario.

A scenario is simply a set of values you use to forecast the outcome of a worksheet model. You can:

- create new scenarios

- switch to and view existing scenarios

- return to the original worksheet values by invoking Undo

Creating a What-If scenario

To revert to the data values which preceded a scenario, press Ctrl+Z immediately after viewing it.

Pull down the Tools menu and do the following:

Click here

...cont'd

Now carry out the following steps:

To amend values in an existing scenario, click this button:

in the Scenario Manager dialog. Now complete the Edit Scenario and Scenario Values dialogs in line with steps 3-7. Finally, perform step 8.

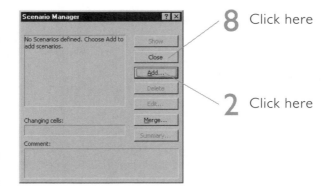

8 Click here

2 Click here

3 Name the scenario

4 Type in the references of the cells you want to vary

5 Click here

6 Type in What-if values

Re step 6 – at first, the existing values display; amend these as appropriate.

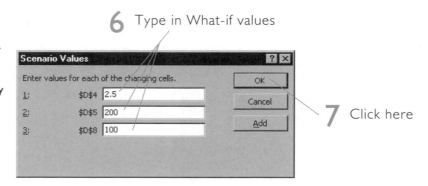

7 Click here

PivotTables

For more information on how to use lists, see chapter 10.

Another technique for reformulating information in a different way is the use of PivotTables. PivotTables provide much greater precision than any of the methods discussed earlier, and they function dynamically.

Using PivotTables

Re step 2 – you can also use external data sources. Click the relevant option and then complete the subsequent dialogs.

1 Click in the relevant list. Pull down the Data menu and click PivotTable and PivotChart Report

2 In the first dialog of the PivotTable and PivotChart Wizard, select 'Microsoft Excel list or database'. Ensure 'PivotTable' is selected, then click Next

3 In the second dialog, click Next

4 In the third and final dialog, select where you want the PivotTable created. Click Finish. The wizard creates the PivotTable within Excel 2000 itself:

Re step 4 – click New worksheet or Existing worksheet. If the latter, enter the reference of the cell which will form the upper-left corner of the PivotTable.

5 Drag any of the fields in the toolbar to the appropriate PivotTable section...

The PivotTable toolbar

PivotTables are dynamic: you can drag any of the existing fields to new locations – or add new ones from the toolbar – all within Excel 2000 worksheets. When you do so, Excel updates the PivotTable accordingly...

The end result:

The new PivotTable

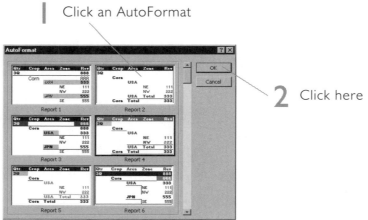

Excel has inserted the relevant totals/sub-totals

Here, three of the fields in the list shown on page 124 – 'Units Used' and 'Unit Price' – have been associated with 'Amount Due'.

You can create charts linked to PivotTable data. Click a cell in the PivotTable. Click this button:

in the Standard toolbar. The new PivotChart is dynamic:

Using PivotTable AutoFormat

You can reformat PivotTables by applying AutoFormats (combinations of formatting characteristics). You can choose from a total of 21.

Click in the PivotTable. Pull down the Format menu and select AutoFormat. Now do the following:

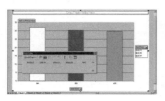

You can reposition fields at will...

| Click an AutoFormat

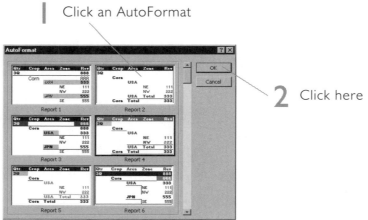

2 Click here

Using lists

This chapter shows you how to create lists/databases in Excel 2000 worksheets. Once created, lists can be sorted in various ways, to make your data more accessible. You can also filter data, so that information you don't want to view is temporarily excluded.

Covers

Chapter Ten

Lists – an overview

In Excel 2000, a list is a series of worksheet rows which contain associated data (e.g. customer or supplier details).

Additionally, lists can function as databases. When they do:

- the list columns become fields

- the column labels act as field names

- each row in the list is a unique record

Column (field) names

Product	Unit Price	Units Used	Amount due	VAT
Electricity	£0.07	425	£29.75	£5.21
Gas	£0.13	246	£31.98	£5.60
Water	£0.08	380	£30.40	£5.32

A simple list

Working with lists

When you've created a list, you can rearrange the data in various ways (Excel 2000 calls this 'sorting'). This is a useful technique. You can sort data:

- in ascending order

- in descending order

- based on the contents of as many as three columns

- based on the contents of rows

Other operations you can carry out on lists/databases include:

- inserting records via data forms

- applying simple filters with the use of AutoFilter

- applying complex filters with the use of criteria

When you create a list, bear the following in mind:

- *use only one list per worksheet*
- *the first row in any list must label the relevant columns*
- *ensure rows have similar values in each column*
- *ensure column names are formatted differently from list data*
- *ensure the list is surrounded by at least one blank row AND one blank column*
- *don't insert blank rows/ columns within the list*
- *don't use spaces at the start or end of list cells*

List sorting

To carry out a sort, click any cell in the relevant list. Pull down the Data menu and click Sort. Then do one of the following:

- to perform a simple sort in ascending or descending order, carry out steps 1-2

- to sort list columns based on row contents, perform steps 3-5 first, then follow steps 1-2 (complete the 'Then by' fields lower down the dialog, as appropriate)

(See also the HOT TIP.)

Finally, carry out step 6:

Click here; select the column you want to sort by

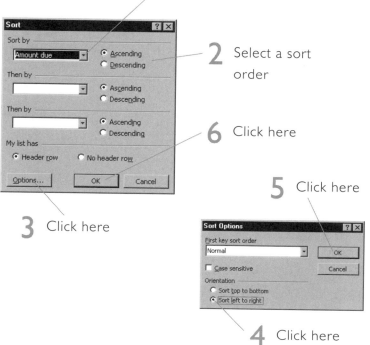

2 Select a sort order

6 Click here

5 Click here

3 Click here

4 Click here

Using AutoFilter

You can use a special Excel 2000 feature – AutoFilter – to display only those list/database rows (records) which contain specific data.

To remove an AutoFilter, pull down the Data menu and click Filter, AutoFilter – the:

against the menu entry disappears.

Applying AutoFilter

Click a cell in the relevant list. Pull down the Data menu and click Filter, AutoFilter. Do the following:

1 In the column you want to filter, click here

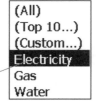

Pr..uct	U..rice	Units Used	Amount due	VAT
Ele..	£0.07	425	£29.75	£5.21
Gas..	..	246	£31.98	£5.60
Water	£0.0.	380	£30.40	£5.32

Repeat steps 1 - 2 on another column, if required.

(All)
(Top 10...)
(Custom...)
Electricity
Gas
Water

2 Click the value you want to display

The end result

This is the result of applying the above AutoFilter:

The following change occurs with columns which have had AutoFilter applied to them:

The arrow turns blue

Product	Unit Price	Units Used	Amount due	VAT
Electricity	£0.07	425	£29.75	£5.21

Applying criteria

The example used here is an instance of one condition applied over more than one column. You can also use several conditions in one column. For example, the following criteria range:

Country
England
France
Netherlands

displays those rows which contain 'England', 'France' or 'Netherlands' in the Country column.

Filters created by AutoFilter are relatively limited – for instance, you can (in effect) only create and view matches with the use of the = comparison operator. You can't use any of Excel 2000's additional operators. (See page 43 for full details of comparison operators.)

You can, however, apply more complex filters with the use of criteria.

Applying criteria

Do the following:

1 Ensure your worksheet has a minimum of three blank rows (or preferably more) over the list you want to filter – the blank rows are known as the 'criteria range'

2 In the list, select the column labels which relate to the values you want to specify as filters. Press Ctrl+C

3 Click in the first blank row of your criteria range. Press Shift+Insert to insert the criteria labels

4 Type in the relevant criteria in the row immediately below the criteria labels:

In the criteria range on the right, all of the following criteria must be true for rows to display:

- the Product must be Gas
- the Unit Price must be greater than £0.09
- fewer than 400 units must have been used

Criteria labels

Product	Unit Price	Units Used		
Gas	>£0.09	<400		
Product	Unit Price	Units Used	Amount due	VAT
Electricity	£0.07	425	£29.75	£5.21
Gas	£0.13	246	£31.98	£5.60
Water	£0.08	380	£30.40	£5.32

The criteria range

Perform the additional steps on page 128.

Now do the following:

5 Click anywhere in the list

6 Pull down the Data menu and click Filter, Advanced Filter

To have Excel 2000 apply the relevant filter in a different location, click Copy to another location:

In the Copy to: field, type in the reference of the cell you want to form the upper-left corner of where you want the filtered rows inserted.

Finally, perform step 8.

7 Type in the criteria range reference (e.g.: B5:D6)

Re step 7 – the criteria range must include the criteria labels to be effective.

8 Click here

The end result

This is the result of applying the advanced filter detailed on page 127:

Product	Unit Price	Units Used		
Gas	>£0.09	<400		
Product	**Unit Price**	**Units Used**	**Amount due**	**VAT**
Gas	£0.13	246	£31.98	£5.60

To remove a filter from a list, pull down the Data menu and click Show All.

Rows which don't match the criteria have been excluded

Multiple worksheets/workbooks

In this chapter, you'll learn how to create new worksheet windows and then rearrange them to best effect. You'll then set up data links between worksheets and workbooks, and create 3D references in formulas. Next, you'll discover how to achieve a useful overview by hiding rows and columns (including the use of outlining). Finally, you'll split worksheets into separate panes (so each can be viewed separately) and freeze them for independent scrolling.

Covers

Chapter Eleven

Viewing several worksheets

Excel 2000 lets you view multiple worksheets simultaneously. This can be particularly useful when they have data in common. Viewing multiple worksheets is a two-stage process:

1. opening a new window

2. selecting the additional worksheet

Opening a new window

Pull down the Window menu and do the following:

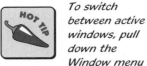

To switch between active windows, pull down the Window menu and click the relevant entry in the list at the bottom.

(Alternatively, click the relevant icon e.g.:

in the Windows Taskbar.)

Click here

Selecting the additional worksheet

Excel now launches a new window showing an alternative view of the active worksheet. Do the following:

If you want to work with alternative views of the same worksheet – a useful technique in itself – simply omit step 2.

2 Click the relevant sheet tab

Rearranging worksheet windows

When you have multiple worksheet windows open at once, you can arrange them in specific patterns. This is a useful technique because it makes worksheets more visible and accessible. The available options are:

Use standard Windows techniques to move, close and resize open windows.

Tiled   Windows are displayed side by side:

Horizontal   Windows are displayed in a tiled column, with horizontal subdivisions:

Vertical   Windows are displayed in a tiled row, with vertical subdivisions:

Cascade   Windows are overlaid with a slight offset:

Rearranging windows

1 Pull down the Window menu and click Arrange

2 In the Arrange Windows dialog, select an arrangement (e.g. Tiled) then click OK

Links within a single workbook

Consider the following examples:

	A	B	C	D	E
1		**Sales Figures 1999**			
2		Qtr1	Qtr2	Qtr3	Qtr4
3		£9,000.00	£11,000.00	£17,000.00	£13,000.00

	A	B	C	D	E
1		**Sales Figures 2000**			
2		Qtr1	Qtr2	Qtr3	Qtr4
3		£10,000.00	£12,000.00	£19,000.00	£14,000.00

Here, we have extracts from two separate worksheets within the same workbook. The first records sales figures for 1999, the second sales figures for 2000. In the excerpts shown, the amount of data is small; there is really no reason why both sets of data shouldn't have been recorded on a single worksheet. However, where you're concerned with large amounts of data, it *is* a very good idea to record them on separate worksheets. By the same token, if you needed to record and collate the totals it would be advantageous to do this on a third worksheet...

You can also set up links between separate workbooks –
see page 134.

Using lots of smaller worksheets (as opposed to a single, much larger sheet) produces the following benefits:

- your worksheets will recalculate faster (because large worksheets are much more unwieldy)

- it's much easier to remain in control of your worksheets

When you do use separate worksheets, you can 'link' the relevant data. To revert to the earlier example, the totals in the third worksheet could be linked to the relevant data in the 1999 Sales and 2000 Sales worksheets. This ensures that, when the contents of any of the relevant cells on the latter worksheets are changed, the totals are automatically updated.

Establishing links

Create the necessary additional worksheet. Then do the following:

This worksheet refers back to the illustrations on page 132.

Select the cell you want to link

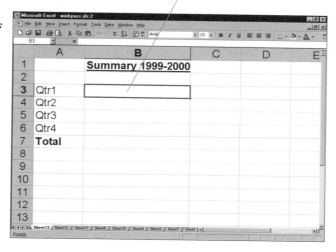

You can have cell references in formulas include worksheet names by separating the name and reference with '!' (but omit the quote marks).

For example, to refer to cell A18 in worksheet 12, type:

Sheet12!A18

within the formula.

Now type in the required formula. Follow these rules:

1.   Type =

2.   Type in the reference to the cell on the first worksheet

3.   Type in the relevant operator – in this case, +

4.   Type in the reference to the cell on the second worksheet

5.   Press Enter

In our specific example (and given that the 1999 totals are on Sheet11 and the 2000 totals on Sheet12), the formula will be:

=Sheet11!B3+Sheet12!B3

Links between workbooks

You can also insert links to other workbooks, either open or on disk. Look at the illustration below:

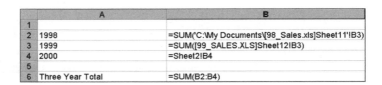

	A	B
1		
2	1998	=SUM('C:\My Documents\[98_Sales.xls]Sheet11'!B3)
3	1999	=SUM([99_SALES.XLS]Sheet12!B3)
4	2000	=Sheet2!B4
5		
6	Three Year Total	=SUM(B2:B4)

This is an excerpt from a new workbook: '2000_Sales.xls'. This, as its name implies, totals sales for the years 1998-2000 inclusive. The formula in B2 is:

=SUM('C:\My Documents\[98_Sales.xls]Sheet11'!B3)

Here, we're instructing Excel 2000 to refer to a workbook called '98_Sales.xls' in the My Documents folder. This workbook isn't currently open. Notice that:

* the full workbook/worksheet address is enclosed in single quotes

* the workbook title is surrounded by square brackets

Use the syntax in the examples given here in your own linking formulas.

Study the formula for B3 below:

=SUM([99_Sales.xls]Sheet12!B3)

Here, we don't need to specify the workbook address (i.e. the drive and folder) because the file is already open. Apart from this, however, the same syntax applies.

And the formula for B4:

=Sheet2!B4

This formula refers to a specific worksheet and cell within the current workbook – 2000_Sales.xls – using the standard techniques we've discussed in earlier chapters.

3D references

In the example discussed on pages 132 and 133, all the worksheets have exactly the same format in that each quarterly amount lies in the same cell on each sheet. When this is the case, you can use an alternative method of summarising the sales figures on the third sheet: 3D referencing. Using 3D references is often quicker and more convenient.

3D references consist of both of the following:

- a sheet range (i.e. the beginning and end sheets are specified, separated by a colon)

- a standard cell range

Not all Excel 2000 functions support 3D referencing. Those that do include:

- *Average*
- *Count*
- *Max*
- *Min*
- *Sum*

Entering a 3D reference

Select the relevant cell. Type in the required formula. As you do so, follow these rules:

1. Type =

2. Type in the appropriate function (see the BEWARE tip), then (

3. Type in the reference to the first worksheet, followed by a colon

4. Type in the reference to the final worksheet

5. Type !

6. Type in the cell range in the normal way, then)

7. Press Enter

In our specific example (and given that the 1999 totals are on Sheet11 and the 2000 totals on Sheet12, both in cell B3), the 3D formula will be:

=Sum(Sheet11:Sheet12!B3)

Hiding data

If a worksheet contains a mass of information, you can temporarily hide some of the data to get an overview.

Hiding rows and columns

Select the row(s) or column(s) to be hidden. Pull down the Format menu and carry out steps 1-2 OR 3-4 below, as appropriate:

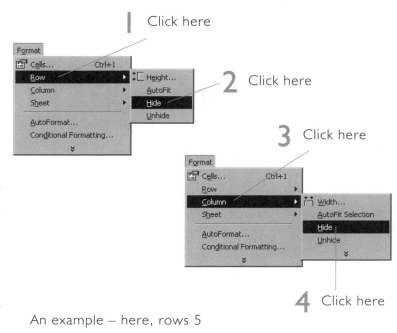

To unhide data, make a selection which includes the row(s) or column(s). (For instance, to unhide rows 5 and 6 in the example on the right, select rows 4-7 inclusive). Pull down the Format menu and click Row, Unhide or Column, Unhide.

An example – here, rows 5 and 6 have been hidden

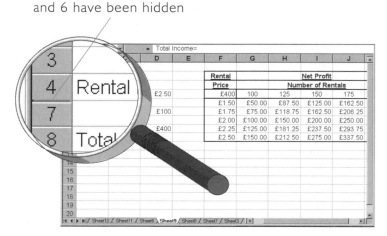

Outlining

Outlines use levels (up to 8) to allow you to expand or collapse sections of a worksheet at will, and are nested (each inner level supplies details of the earlier outer one).

An alternative way to hide rows or columns temporarily is to outline (or group) them. When you apply outlining to specific data within a worksheet, Excel 2000 inserts an Outline Level Bar against it. You can then specify whether the data displays or not.

Applying outlining

Select one or more rows or columns containing the data you want to outline. Pull down the Data menu and do the following:

You can only apply outlining to lists. (For more on lists, see Chapter 10.)

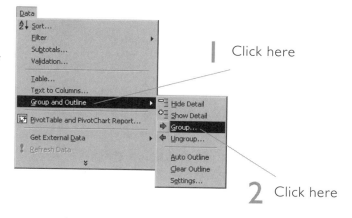

1 Click here

2 Click here

To hide the Outline Level bar, pull down the Tools menu and click Options; activate the View tab and deselect Outline symbols.

The end result

In the example below, rows 3-6 have been outlined, and will be hidden (see page 138):

The range F3:F6 has also been grouped.

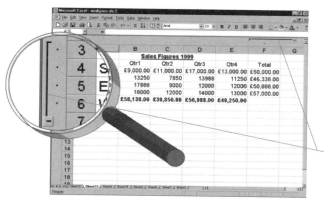

The Outline Level Bar – see page 138

Hiding outlined data

To hide data which you've outlined, do the following:

In outlinable lists, summary rows (i.e. those which contain totals) must be below the list data, while summary columns must be to the right.

Click here

You can also hide or unhide data levels by referring to the row or column level symbols below the Name box. Do the following:

Unhiding outlined data

To unhide data which you've outlined, do the following:

Click the smaller number(s) to hide data, the larger numbers to reveal it

Click here

In this example, it wasn't possible to select rows 2-7 en masse, since doing so would only have removed the outline over column F...

Instead, the cells which relate to the hidden rows were selected.

Removing outlines

If you want to remove an outline, make a selection which includes the appropriate row(s) or column(s). In the illustration below, rows 3-6 have previously been outlined and are currently hidden; to remove this outlining, cells A2:E7 have been selected (see the DON'T FORGET tip):

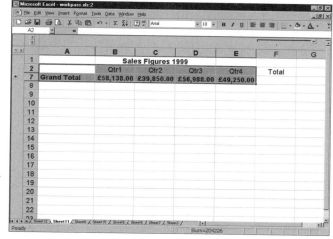

If you pre-select a cell range (as here) rather than one or more whole rows or columns, Excel 2000 may launch a further dialog after step 2.

Do the following:

A Make the relevant selection

B Click here

Now pull down the Data menu and do the following:

Click here

2 Click here

Splitting worksheets

Excel 2000 has two further techniques you can use to make complex worksheets easier to understand. You can:

- split worksheets horizontally or vertically into panes

- freeze individual panes, so that the data they contain doesn't scroll

In the example shown here, row 6 was selected before step 1 was performed; as a result, Excel has inserted the Split Bar below row 5.

Splitting worksheets

Select the row or column before which you want the worksheet to be split. Pull down the Window menu and do the following:

Click here

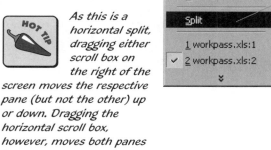

As this is a horizontal split, dragging either scroll box on the right of the screen moves the respective pane (but not the other) up or down. Dragging the horizontal scroll box, however, moves both panes to the right or left.

(With vertical splits, the vertical scroll box moves both panes, while the horizontal scroll boxes are pane-specific.)

The Split Bar   The Two panes

	B	C	D	E	F	G	H	I	J	K	L
1											
2	Video Rentals				Rental			Net Profit			
3					Price			Number of Rentals			
4	Rental Price=		2.5		£400	100	125	150	175	200	
5	Number of Rentals=		200		£1.00	£0.00	£25.00	£50.00	£75.00	£100.00	
6	Total Income=		£500		£1.25	£25.00	£56.25	£87.50	£118.75	£150.00	
7					£1.50	£50.00	£87.50	£125.00	£162.50	£200.00	
8	Total Costs=		£100		£1.75	£75.00	£118.75	£162.50	£206.25	£250.00	
9					£2.00	£100.00	£150.00	£200.00	£250.00	£300.00	
10	Net Profit=		£400		£2.25	£125.00	£181.25	£237.50	£293.75	£350.00	
11					£2.50	£150.00	£212.50	£275.00	£337.50	£400.00	
12											
13											

Freezing worksheets

Do one of the following, as appropriate:

1.	To create two panes with the top pane frozen, select the row above which you want the split inserted

2.	To create two panes with the left pane frozen, select the column to the left of which you want the split inserted

3.	To create four panes with the upper and left panes frozen, select the cell to the right of, and below, where you want the split inserted

Now pull down the Window menu and do the following:

Create the precise effect you need by using split and freeze combinations.

Here, column E was selected before the worksheet was frozen, thereby creating a vertical freeze.
Dragging the horizontal scroll bar moves only the right-hand pane to the left or right but has no effect on the left-hand pane. On the other hand, the effect of dragging the vertical scroll bar is unchanged (both panes move up or down). This situation is reversed for horizontal freezes.

Click here

The Freeze split

	A	B	C	D	E	F	G	H	I	J	K
1											
2		Video Rentals				Rental			Net Profit		
3						Price			Number of Rentals		
4		Rental Price=		2.5		£400	100	125	150	175	200
5		Number of Rentals=		200		£1.00	£0.00	£25.00	£50.00	£75.00	£100.0(
6		Total Income=		£500		£1.25	£25.00	£56.25	£87.50	£118.75	£150.0(
7						£1.50	£50.00	£87.50	£125.00	£162.50	£200.0(
8		Total Costs=		£100		£1.75	£75.00	£118.75	£162.50	£206.25	£250.0(
9						£2.00	£100.00	£150.00	£200.00	£250.00	£300.0(
10		Net Profit=		£400		£2.25	£125.00	£181.25	£237.50	£293.75	£350.0(
11						£2.50	£150.00	£212.50	£275.00	£337.50	£400.0(
12											

Window menu:
New Window
Arrange...
Hide
Unhide...
Split
Freeze Panes
1 workpass2.xls:1
✓ 2 workpass2.xls:2

Adjusting worksheet splits

Redefining a split

You can adjust a split with the use of the mouse. Move the mouse pointer over the Split Bar – it changes to: ⯮

Re step 1 –
you can't use
this technique
with frozen
worksheets.

Now carry out the following:

Drag the Split Bar to a new location

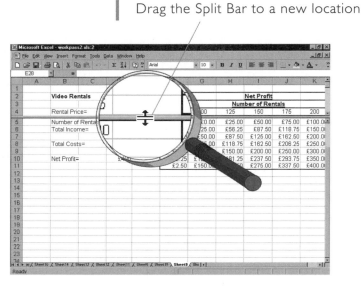

You can't
remove splits in
frozen
worksheets by
double-clicking
them.
   Instead, pull down the
Window menu and click
Remove Split (this also
unfreezes the relevant
panes).

Removing a split

To remove a split, simply double-click the Split Bar.

Unfreezing a worksheet

Pull down the Window menu and do the following:

Click here

Formatting worksheets

In this chapter, you'll learn to customise cell formatting. You'll specify how cell contents align, apply fonts and type sizes and border/fill cells. You'll also format data automatically, and transfer formats between cells. Then you'll use conditional formatting to have Excel flag cells which meet specific criteria. Finally, you'll carry out data searches and use styles to make formatting even easier.

Covers

Chapter Twelve

Cell alignment

By default, Excel 2000 aligns text to the left of cells, and numbers to the right. However, if you want you can change this.

You can specify alignment under two broad headings: Horizontal and Vertical.

Horizontal alignment

One further horizontal option – Center Across Selection – centres cell contents across more than one cell (if you selected a cell range before initiating it).

The main options are:

General	the default (see above)
Left	the contents are aligned from the left
Center	the contents are centred
Right	the contents are aligned from the right
Fill	the contents are duplicated so that they fill the cell
Justify	a combination of Left and Right

Vertical alignment

You can also rotate text within cells – see page 145 for more information.

Available options are:

Top	cell contents align with the top of the cell(s)
Center	the contents are centred
Bottom	the contents align with the cell bottom
Justify	the contents are aligned along the top and bottom of the cell(s)

Most of these settings parallel features found in Word 2000 (and many other word-processors). The difference, however, lies in the fact that Excel 2000 has to align data within the bounds of cells rather than a page. When it aligns text, it often needs to employ its own version of text wrap. See page 145 for more information on this.

...cont'd

Other alignments you can set are rotation and text wrap.

Rotation controls the direction of text flow within cells; you achieve this by specifying a plus (anticlockwise) or minus (clockwise) angle.

When the Wrap Text option is selected, Excel – instead of overflowing any surplus text into adjacent cells to the right – forces it onto separate lines within the host cell.

	A	B	C
1	Here, text wrap is not in force		
2			
3			
4			
5	This text, however, *has* been wrapped		

Text wrap in action

Customising cell alignment

Select the cell(s) whose contents you want to realign. Pull down the Format menu and click Cells. Carry out step 1 below. Follow steps 2-4, as appropriate. Finally, carry out step 5.

Ensure the Alignment tab is active

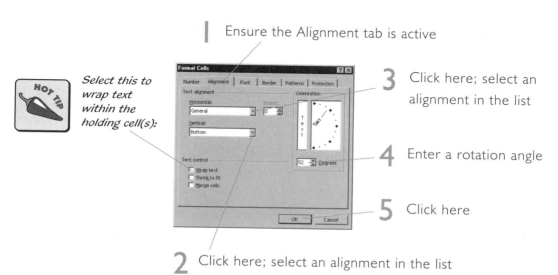

Select this to wrap text within the holding cell(s):

3 Click here; select an alignment in the list

4 Enter a rotation angle

5 Click here

2 Click here; select an alignment in the list

Changing fonts and styles

Don't confuse font styles with overall styles (collections of formatting aspects).

See pages 154-158 for how to use overall styles.

Excel lets you carry out the following actions on cell contents (numbers and/or text). You can:

- apply a new font and/or type size

- apply a font style (for most fonts, you can choose from: Regular, Italic, Bold or Bold Italic)

- apply a colour

- apply a special effect: <u>underlining</u>, ~~strikethrough~~, superscript or subscript

Amending the appearance of cell contents

Select the cell(s) whose contents you want to reformat. Pull down the Format menu and click Cells. Carry out step 1 below. Now follow any of steps 2-5, as appropriate, or either or both of the HOT TIPS. Finally, carry out step 6.

To underline the specified contents, click the arrow to the right of the Underline box; select an underlining type in the list.

To apply a special effect, click any of the options in the Effects section.

Ensure the Font tab is active

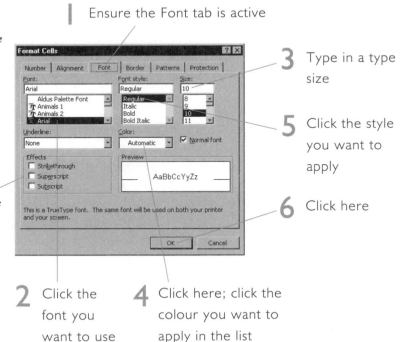

3 Type in a type size

5 Click the style you want to apply

6 Click here

2 Click the font you want to use

4 Click here; click the colour you want to apply in the list

Bordering cells

Excel 2000 lets you define a border around:

- the perimeter of a selected cell range

- specific sides within a cell range

You can customise the border by choosing from a selection of pre-defined border styles. You can also add new line styles to specific sides, or colour the border.

Applying a cell border

First, select the cell range you want to border. Pull down the Format menu and click Cells. Now carry out step 1 below. Follow step 2 to apply an overall border. Carry out step 3 if you want to deactivate one or more border sides. Perform step 4 if you want to colour the border. Finally, carry out step 5:

If you want to customise the border style, click a line style here:

immediately after step 2. Omit step 3. Follow step 4 if you want to colour the new style. Now do the following in this part of the dialog:

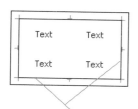

Click any of the 4 borders to apply the new style

Finally, carry out step 5.

1 Ensure the Border tab is active

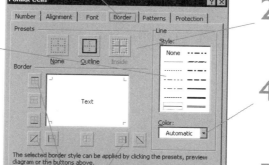

2 Click the relevant border style option

4 Optional – click here and select a colour in the list

5 Click here

3 Optional – click a border option to deselect it

Shading cells

Excel 2000 lets you apply the following to cells:

• a background colour

• a foreground pattern

• a foreground colour

Interesting effects can be achieved by using pattern and colour combinations with coloured backgrounds.

Applying a pattern or background

First, select the cell range you want to shade. Pull down the Format menu and click Cells. Now carry out step 1. Perform step 2 to apply a background colour, and/or 3-5 to apply a foreground pattern or a pattern/colour combination. Finally, follow step 6.

Ensure the Patterns tab is active

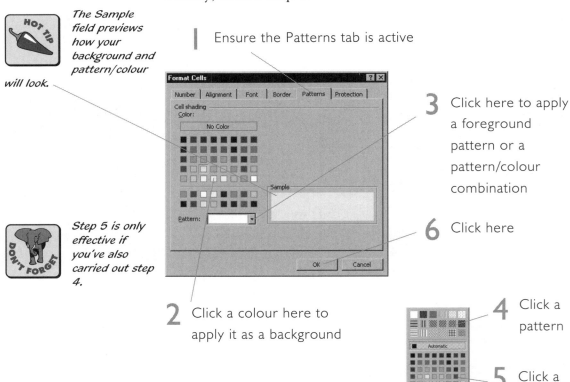

3 Click here to apply a foreground pattern or a pattern/colour combination

6 Click here

2 Click a colour here to apply it as a background

4 Click a pattern

5 Click a colour

AutoFormat

Excel 2000 provides a shortcut to the formatting of worksheet data: AutoFormat.

AutoFormat consists of 16 pre-defined formatting schemes. These incorporate specific excerpts from the font, alignment, border and shading options discussed earlier. You can apply any of these schemes (and their associated formatting) to selected cell ranges with just a few mouse clicks. You can even specify which scheme elements you don't wish to use.

AutoFormat works with most arrangements of worksheet data.

Using AutoFormat

First, select the cell range you want to apply an automatic format to. Pull down the Format menu and click AutoFormat. Now carry out step 1 below. Steps 2-3 are optional. Finally, follow step 4:

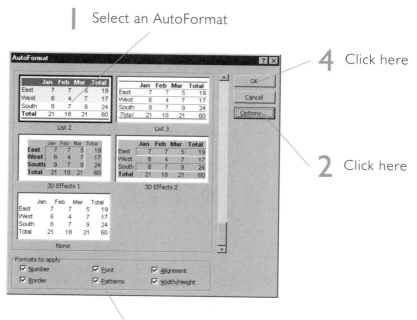

Select an AutoFormat

4 Click here

2 Click here

3 Click one or more options to omit them

The Format Painter

Re. step 1 – double-click the Format Painter icon if you want to apply the selected formatting more than once. Then repeat step 2 as often as needed.

Press Esc when you've finished.

Excel 2000 provides a very useful tool which can save you a lot of time and effort: the Format Painter. You can use the Format Painter to copy the formatting attributes from cells you've previously formatted to other cells, in one operation.

Using the Format Painter

First, apply the necessary formatting, if you haven't already done so. Then select the formatted cells. Refer to the Standard toolbar and do the following:

Click the Format Painter icon

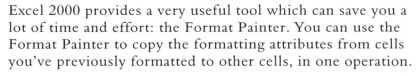

Re step 1 – if you haven't used it much (or if you've expanded the Formatting toolbar), the Format Painter button may be on the Standard toolbar fly-out instead. If it is, click:

to access it.

Pre-formatted text

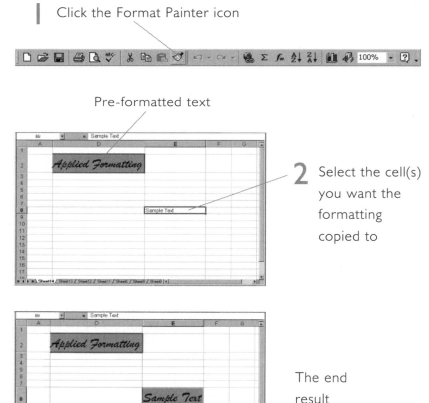

Select the cell(s) you want the formatting copied to

The end result

When you've finished using the Format Painter (or before, if you decide you don't want to proceed), press Esc.

Conditional formatting

Formatting which alters cell size (e.g. font changes) can't be used as a conditional format.

You can have Excel 2000 apply conditional formats to specific cells. Conditional formats are formatting attributes (e.g. colour or shading) which Excel imposes on cells when the criteria you set are met. Conditional formats help you identify cells and monitor worksheets.

For instance, in a worksheet in which B10 is the total of the number of videos rented out, you could tell Excel 2000 to colour B10 in red if the value it contains falls below a certain level, or in blue if it exceeds it...

Applying conditional formatting

Select the relevant cell(s). Pull down the Format menu and click Conditional Formatting. Now do the following:

If you want, you can use a TRUE/FALSE formula to define the match.
Click here:
Select Formula Is. Now type in the formula in the field to the right. Finally, carry out steps 3-7, as appropriate.

1 Click here; select a comparison phrase

2 Type in a match value

3 Click here

7 Click here

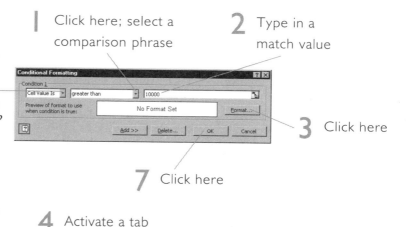

Re step 2 – complete more than one field, if necessary (in line with the comparison phrase chosen).

4 Activate a tab

5 Select the appropriate formatting

6 Click here

Re step 5 – the available options depend on the tab selected in step 4.

Find operations

Excel 2000 lets you search for and jump to text or numbers (in short, any information) in your worksheets. This is a particularly useful feature when worksheets become large and complex.

You can organise your search by rows or by columns. You can also specify whether Excel looks in:

- cells that contain formulas

- cells that don't contain formulas

Additionally, you can insist that Excel only flag exact matches (i.e. if you searched for '11', Excel would not find '1111'), and you can also limit text searches to text which has the case you specified (e.g. searching for 'PRODUCT LIST' would not find 'Product List' or 'product list').

To search for data over more than one worksheet, select the relevant sheet tabs before launching the Find dialog.

Searching for data

Place the mouse pointer at the location in the active worksheet from which you want the search to begin. Pull down the Edit menu and click Find. Now carry out step 1 below, then any of steps 2-5. Finally, carry out step 6.

If you want to restrict the search to specific cells, select a cell range before you launch the Find dialog.

| Type in the data you want to find

4 Click here for a case-specific search

6 Click here

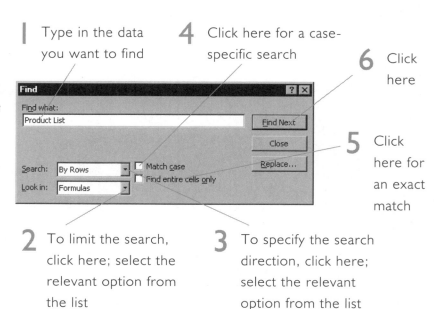

5 Click here for an exact match

2 To limit the search, click here; select the relevant option from the list

3 To specify the search direction, click here; select the relevant option from the list

Find-and-replace operations

When you search for data, you can also – if you want – have Excel 2000 replace it with something else.

Find-and-replace operations can be organised by rows or columns. However, unlike straight searches, you can't specify whether Excel looks in cells that contain formulas or not. As with straight searches, you can, however, limit find-and-replace operations to exact matches and also (in the case of text) to precise case matches.

Normally, find-and-replace operations only affect the host worksheet. If you want to carry out an operation over multiple worksheets, see the HOT TIP.

Running a find-and-replace operation

Place the mouse pointer at the location in the active worksheet from which you want the search to begin (or select a cell range if you want to restrict the find-and-replace operation to this). Pull down the Edit menu and click Replace. Now carry out steps 1-3 below. Finally, carry out step 4 as often as required, or perform step 5 once for a global substitution.

1 Type in the data you want to find

3 Click here to find the 1st occurrence

4 Click here to replace it

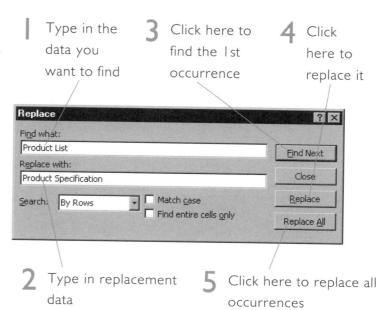

2 Type in replacement data

5 Click here to replace all occurrences

Styles – an overview

Styles are named collections of associated formatting commands.

The advantage of using styles is that you can apply more than one formatting enhancement to selected cells in one go. Once a style is in place, you can change one or more elements of it and have Excel 2000 apply the amendments automatically throughout the whole of the active workbook.

Generally, new workbooks you create in Excel 2000 have the following pre-defined styles as a minimum:

Comma	Only includes numeric formatting – numerals are shown with two decimal places
Comma (0)	Only includes numeric formatting – numerals are shown with 0 decimal places
Currency	Only includes numeric formatting – numerals are shown with two decimal places and the default currency symbol
Currency (0)	Only includes numeric formatting – numerals are shown with 0 decimal places and the default currency symbol
Normal	The default. Includes numeric, alignment, font and border/shading formatting – numerals are shown with 0 decimal places
Percent	Only includes numeric formatting – data is expressed as a percentage

You can easily create (and apply) your own styles.

Creating a style

The easiest way to create a style is to:

A.   apply the appropriate formatting enhancements to one or more specific cells and then select them

B.   tell Excel 2000 to create a new style based on this formatting

First, carry out A. above. Then pull down the Format menu and do the following:

Keep styles simple. Select only single cells or cells with identical formatting.

(Styles are not suitable for ranges of cells with different outline borders.)

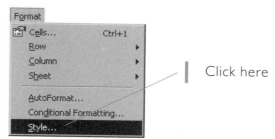

| Click here

2 Type in the new style's name

When you've finished using the Style dialog, click this button:

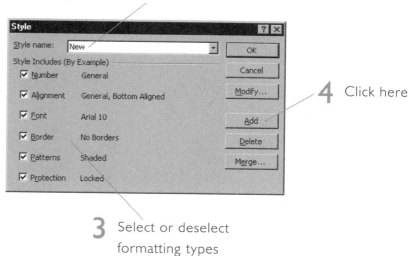

4 Click here

3 Select or deselect formatting types

See page 156 for how to use your new style.

Applying styles

Excel 2000 makes applying styles easy.

First, select the cell(s) you want to apply the style to. Pull down the Format menu and click Style. Now do the following:

Click here; in the list, click the style you want to apply

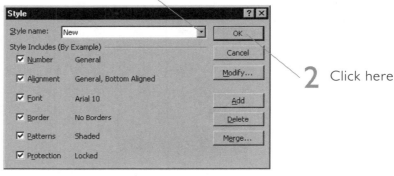

2 Click here

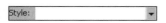

Shortcut for applying styles

Excel makes it even easier to apply styles if you currently have the Formatting toolbar on-screen. (If you haven't, pull down the View menu and click Toolbars, Formatting.)

Select the cell(s) you want to apply the style to. Then do the following:

The Style box   Click here

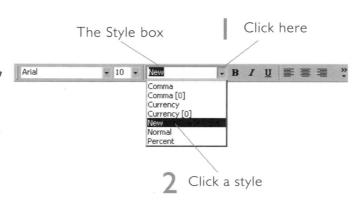

2 Click a style

Amending styles

The easiest way to modify an existing style is to:

When a style is redefined, the changes are restricted to the current workbook.

A. apply the appropriate formatting enhancements to one or more cells and then select them

B. use the Style dialog to select a style and tell Excel to assign the selected formatting to it

First, carry out A. above. Then pull down the Format menu and do the following:

Re step 2 – you must type in the name of the style you want to amend.

(You can't click the ▼ button to the right of the Style name field and select the style from the list.)

Click here

2 Type in the name of the style you want to amend

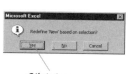

After step 3, a special message launches. Do the following:

Click here

Now click this button:

in the Style dialog.

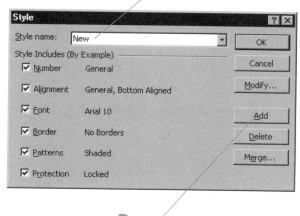

3 Click here

Deleting and copying styles

Good housekeeping sometimes makes it necessary to remove unwanted styles from the active document. Excel 2000 lets you do this very easily.

Another useful feature is the ability to copy ('merge') styles from one workbook to another.

If the workbook you're copying from has styles with the same name as the target workbook, those in the target are overwritten (unless you halt the merge operation).

Deleting styles

Pull down the Format menu and click Style. Now carry out the following steps:

Click here; in the list, click the style you want to delete

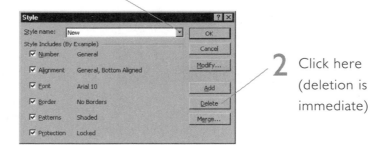

2 Click here (deletion is immediate)

After step 1, below right, Excel 2000 launches the Merge Styles dialog. Do the following:

Double-click the workbook which contains the styles you want to copy

Excel now imports the styles.

Copying styles

Open the workbook from which you want to copy styles, then the workbook you want to copy them into. Pull down the Format menu and click Styles. Now do the following:

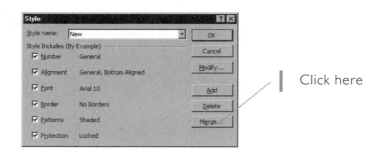

Click here

Printing worksheets

In this chapter, you'll learn how to prepare your worksheets for printing. This involves specifying the paper size and orientation, margins and page numbering, and also defining headers/footers. Then you'll launch and use Print Preview mode, to proof your worksheets. Finally, you'll specify which worksheet components should be printed, and how.

Covers

Chapter Thirteen

Page setup – an overview

Making sure your worksheets print with the correct page setup can be a complex issue, for the simple reason that most worksheets become very extensive with the passage of time (so large, in fact, that in the normal course of things they won't fit onto a single page).

Page setup features you can customise include:

Excel 2000 has a special view mode – Page Break Preview – which you can also use to ensure your worksheet prints correctly.

Pull down the View menu and click Page Break Preview. Do the following (the white area denotes cells which will print, the grey those which won't):

- the paper size and orientation
- scaling
- the starting page number
- the print quality
- margins
- header/footer information
- page order
- which worksheet components print

Margin settings you can amend are:

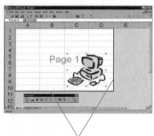

Drag page break margins to customise the printable area

(To leave Page Break Preview when you've finished with it, click Normal in the View menu.)

- top
- bottom
- left
- right

Additionally, you can set the distance between the top page edge and the top of the header, and the distance between the bottom page edge and the bottom edge of the footer.

When you save your active workbook, all Page Setup settings are saved with it.

(Charts in separate chart sheets have unique page setup options – see Chapter 14.)

Setting worksheet options

The Page Setup dialog for charts in chart sheets has a special tab – see chapter 14 for how to use this.

Excel 2000 lets you:

- define a printable area on-screen

- define a column or row title which will print on every page

- specify which worksheet components should print

- print with minimal formatting

- determine the print direction

Using the Sheet tab in the Page Setup dialog

Pull down the File menu and click Page Setup. Now carry out step 1 below, followed by steps 2-4 (and the tips) as appropriate. Finally, carry out step 5.

If you want to print a specific cell range (Print area), type in the address here:

│ Ensure the Sheet tab is active

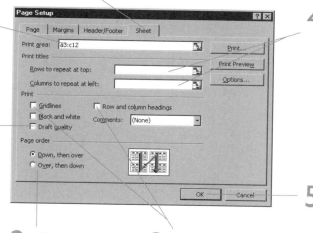

Click Draft Quality for rapid printing with the minimum of formatting.

4 Type in the address of the row/column you want to use as a consistent title

5 Click here

2 Click a direction option

3 Click a component to include or exclude it

Setting page options

Excel 2000 comes with 17 pre-defined paper sizes which you can apply to your worksheets, in either portrait (top-to-bottom) or landscape (sideways on) orientation. This is one approach to effective printing. Another is scaling: you can print out your worksheets as they are, or you can have Excel shrink them so that they fit a given paper size (you can even automate this process). Additionally, you can set the print resolution and starting page number.

Using the Page tab in the Page Setup dialog

Pull down the File menu and click Page Setup. Now carry out step 1 below, followed by steps 2-6 as appropriate. Finally, carry out step 7:

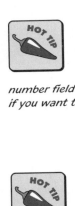

Re step 5 – by default, Excel numbers pages from '1'. Leave the First page number field setting as Auto if you want this.

To make your worksheet print in a specific number of pages, complete the Fit to fields.

1 Ensure the Page tab is active

2 Click the orientation you need

3 Click here; click the page size you need in the drop-down list

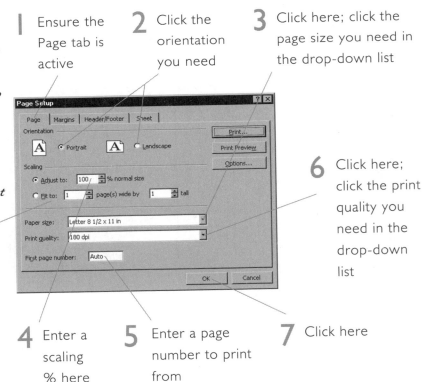

6 Click here; click the print quality you need in the drop-down list

4 Enter a scaling % here

5 Enter a page number to print from

7 Click here

Setting margin options

Excel inserts page breaks automatically. If you need to override these, click the row, column or cell where you want the new page to begin. Pull down the Insert menu and click Page Break.

Excel 2000 lets you set a variety of margin settings. The illustration below shows the main ones:

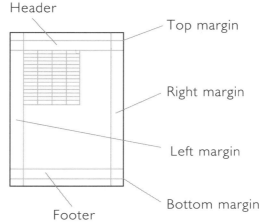

Header

Top margin

Right margin

Left margin

Bottom margin

Footer

To view automatic page breaks, pull down the Tools menu and click Options. Activate the View tab. Ensure Page breaks is selected. Click OK.

Using the Margins tab in the Page Setup dialog

Pull down the File menu and click Page Setup. Now carry out step 1 below, followed by steps 2-3 as appropriate. Finally, carry out step 4:

Ensure the Margins tab is active

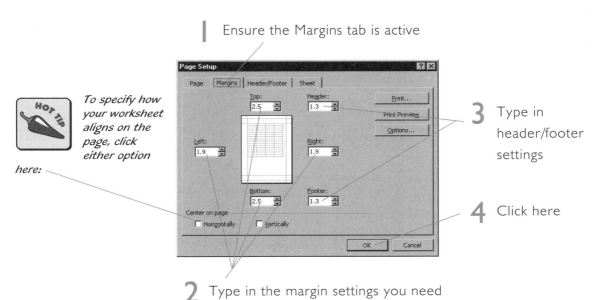

To specify how your worksheet aligns on the page, click either option here:

3 Type in header/footer settings

4 Click here

2 Type in the margin settings you need

Setting header/footer options

Excel 2000 provides a list of built-in header and footer settings. You can apply any of these to the active worksheet. These settings include:

Note that you can also use specific groups of these, for instance:

- *Page 1, Book 1*
- *Confidential, Sheet 1, Page 1*

- the worksheet title

- the workbook title

- the page number

- the user's name

- 'Confidential'

- the date

Using the Header/Footer tab in the Page Setup dialog

Pull down the File menu and click Page Setup. Now carry out step 1 below, followed by steps 2-3 as appropriate. Finally, carry out step 4:

| Ensure the Header/ Footer tab is active

2 Click here; select a header from the list

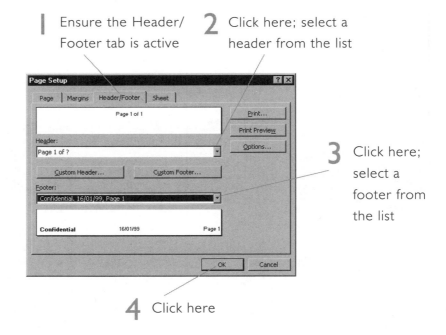

3 Click here; select a footer from the list

4 Click here

Launching Print Preview

Print Preview displays data in greyscale (rather than colour).

Excel 2000 provides a special view mode called Print Preview. This displays the active worksheet exactly as it will look when printed. Use Print Preview as a final check just before you begin printing.

You can perform the following actions from within Print Preview:

Excel 2000's Print Preview mode has only two Zoom settings. These are:

- *Full Page*
- *High-Magnification*

- moving from page to page

- zooming in or out on the active page

- adjusting most Page Setup settings

- adjusting margins visually

Launching Print Preview

Pull down the File menu and click Print Preview. This is the result:

To leave Print Preview mode and return to your worksheet (or chart sheet), simply press Esc.

Special Print Preview toolbar

See Chapter 14 for how to work with charts.

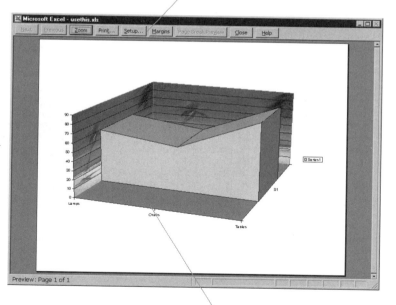

A preview of a chart sheet

Working with Print Preview

All of the operations you can perform in Print Preview mode can be accessed via the toolbar.

Click the Page Break Preview button to launch Page Break Preview – see the HOT TIP on page 160 for how to use it.

Using the Print Preview toolbar

Do any of the following, as appropriate:

1 Click here to jump to the next page

3 Click here to zoom in or out

6 Click here to launch the Page Setup dialog

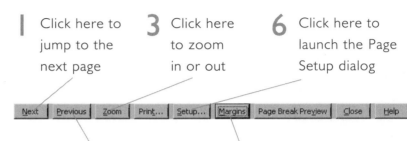

Next   Previous   Zoom   Print...   Setup...   Margins   Page Break Preview   Close   Help

Re step 6 – see earlier topics (pages 160-164) for how to use the Page Setup dialog.

2 Click here to jump to the previous page

4 Click here to toggle margin markers on or off – then follow step 5

5 Drag any margin to reposition it

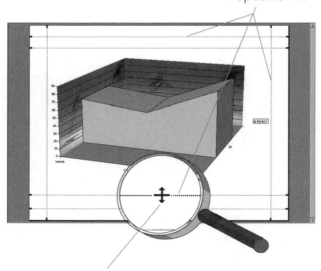

Magnified view of Move pointer

Printing worksheet data

Excel 2000 lets you specify:

• the number of copies you want printed

• whether you want the copies 'collated'. This is the process whereby Excel prints one full copy at a time. For instance, if you're printing three copies of a 10-page worksheet, Excel prints pages 1-10 of the first copy, followed by pages 1-10 of the second and pages 1-10 of the third.

• which pages (or page ranges) you want printed

• whether you want the print run restricted to cells you selected before initiating printing

You can 'mix and match' these, as appropriate.

To select and print more than one worksheet, hold down Shift as you click on multiple tabs in the Worksheet Tab area.

Starting a print run

Open the workbook that contains the data you want to print. If you want to print an entire worksheet, click the relevant tab in the worksheet Tab area. If you need to print a specific cell range within a worksheet, select it. Then pull down the File menu and click Print. Do any of steps 1-5. Then carry out step 6 to begin printing.

Click here; select the printer you want from the list

To adjust your printer's internal settings before you initiate printing, click Properties: Then refer to your printer's manual.

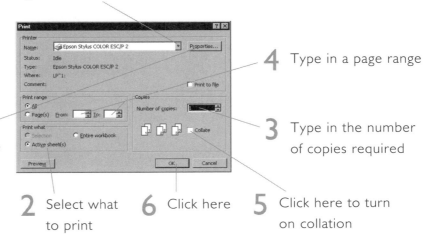

4 Type in a page range

3 Type in the number of copies required

2 Select what to print

6 Click here

5 Click here to turn on collation

Printing – the fast-track approach

There are occasions when you'll merely want to print out your work:

- without having to invoke the Print dialog

- with the current settings applying

- with a single mouse click

One reason for doing this is proofing. Irrespective of how thoroughly you check documents on-screen, there will always be errors and deficiencies which, with the best will in the world, are difficult or impossible to pick up. By initiating printing with the minimum of delay, you can check your work that much more rapidly...

For this reason, Excel 2000 provides a printing method which is especially quick and easy to use.

Printing with the current print options

First, ensure your printer is ready and on-line. Make sure the Standard toolbar is visible. (If it isn't, pull down the View menu and click Toolbars, Standard). Now do the following:

Click here

Excel 2000 starts printing the active worksheet immediately.

Charts and graphics

Use this chapter to learn how to create and insert new charts (both as objects within worksheets and as separate chart sheets) in order to give visual expression to your data, then save your charts to the Internet/Intranets. You'll also insert pictures into your worksheets, then manipulate them. Finally, you'll insert AutoShapes, extraordinarily flexible graphic shapes. All of these techniques improve worksheet impact dramatically.

Covers

Chapter Fourteen

Charting – an overview

You can add a picture or clip art to chart walls. Select the wall(s) in the normal way. Then follow the procedures set out on pages 177-178.

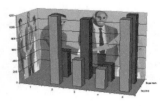

Excel 2000 has comprehensive charting capabilities. You can have it convert selected data into its visual equivalent. To do this, Excel offers a wide number of chart formats and sub-formats.

You can create a chart:

• as a picture within the parent worksheet

• as a separate chart sheet

Chart sheets have their own tabs in the Tab area; these operate just like worksheet tabs.

Excel uses a special Wizard – the Chart Wizard – to make the process of creating charts as easy and convenient as possible.

When you resize a chart, fonts rescale automatically, for increased legibility.

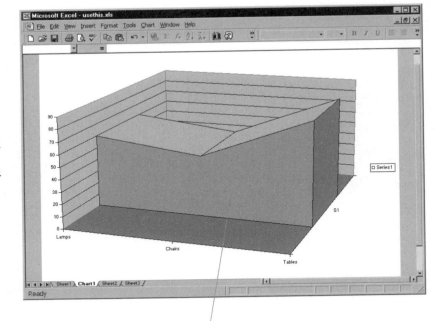

A 3-D Area chart, in a separate chart sheet

Creating a chart

First, select the cells you want converted into a chart. Pull down the Insert menu and click Chart. The first Chart Wizard dialog appears. Do the following:

Click a chart type

To have Excel preview the selected chart combination in the Chart sub-type field, click and hold here:

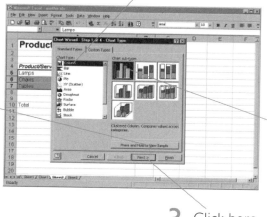

2 Click a chart sub-type

3 Click here

Re step 4 – note the following. You can click the Collapse Dialog button:

to hide the dialog temporarily while you select an alternative cell range. When you've finished, do the following:

Click here

There are three more dialogs to complete. Carry out the following steps:

4 If you selected the wrong cells before launching the Chart Wizard, click here; then carry out the procedures in the HOT TIP

The Collapse Dialog button

5 Click here

Click any of the additional tabs to set further chart options. For example, activate the Gridlines tab to specify how and where gridlines display. Or click Legend to determine where legends (text labels) display...

Excel 2000 now launches the third Chart Wizard dialog. Carry out the following additional steps:

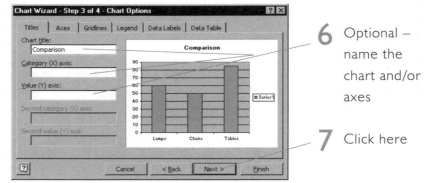

6 Optional – name the chart and/or axes

7 Click here

In the final dialog, you tell Excel whether you want the chart inserted into the current worksheet, or into a new chart sheet.

Carry out step 8 OR 9 below. Finally, perform step 10.

To convert an existing chart to a new type, select it. Pull down the Chart menu and click Chart Type. Now follow steps 1-3 on page 171.
Alternatively, you can apply a custom chart type. Launch the Chart Type dialog (as above). Activate the Custom Types tab. In the Chart type: field, click a custom type. Click OK.

8 Click here to create a chart sheet

9 Click here; select an existing sheet in the list

10 Click here to generate the chart

Formatting charts

To add text to a chart, click it. Type in the text; press Enter. Excel 2000 places it near the centre of the chart; drag the text to the correct location.

To amend the formatting of a chart component, do the following:

1 Double-click the component you want to format

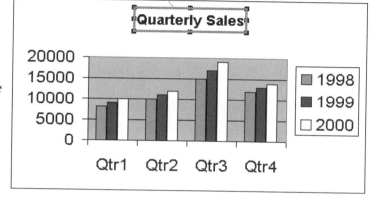

You can rotate text along chart axes. To do this, double-click the text frame e.g.:

Quarterly Sales

Frame

In the dialog, click the Alignment tab. Type in a plus or minus rotation in the Degrees field. Click OK.

2 Activate the relevant tab

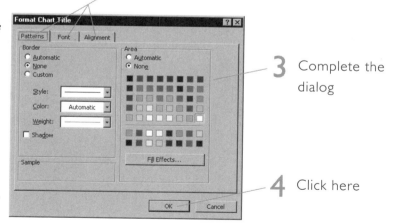

3 Complete the dialog

If you aren't sure what a chart component refers to, move the mouse pointer over it; Excel displays an explanatory Chart Tip e.g.:

4 Click here

Value Axis

Page setup for charts

Most page setup issues for charts are identical to those for worksheet data (see page 161). The main difference, however, is that the Page Setup dialog has a Chart (rather than a Sheet) tab.

In the Chart tab, you can opt to have the chart:

- printed at full size

- scaled to fit the page

- user-defined

You can also set the print quality.

See Chapter 13 for detailed advice on how to print worksheets and charts.

Using the Chart tab in the Page Setup dialog

Select the relevant chart or chart sheet. Pull down the File menu and click Page Setup. Now carry out step 1 below, followed by steps 2-3 as appropriate. Finally, carry out step 4.

Re step 3 – clicking Custom ensures that, when you return to the chart sheet, the chart size can be adjusted with the mouse in the normal way. The chart then prints at whatever size you set.

| Ensure the Chart tab is active

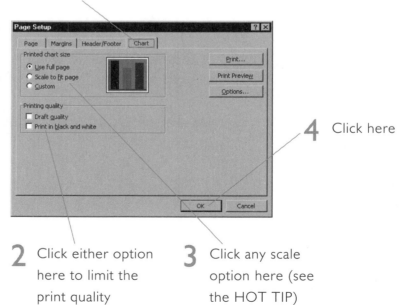

4 Click here

2 Click either option here to limit the print quality

3 Click any scale option here (see the HOT TIP)

Saving charts to the Web

To publish your charts on the Web, you must have a live Internet connection.

You can publish your charts (either as chart sheets, or as charts embedded in worksheets) to the Internet or Intranets. This produces HTML files which can be viewed in more or less any browser, without the need to have access to Excel 2000. You can publish charts non-interactively or interactively.

(See page 60 for details of non-interactive v. interactive publishing.)

Publishing interactive charts

Select the relevant chart or chart sheet. Pull down the File menu and do the following:

Refer to (and implement where appropriate) steps 1-7 on page 61 before you carry out the procedures discussed here.

(Pay particular attention to step 1.)

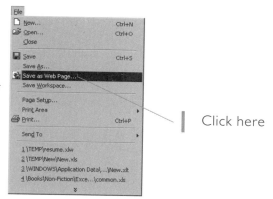

Click here

If you want to save a chart non-interactively, first select it. Carry out the relevant procedures on page 63 (after step 1, however, ensure that Selection: Chart is activated).

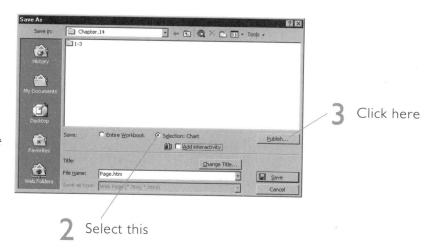

3 Click here

2 Select this

...cont'd

Now carry out the following additional steps:

4 Optional – click here; in the list, select the type of data you want to publish

5 Optional – specify a data item

To preview your chart in your browser, select 'Open published Web page in browser' before you carry out step 11.

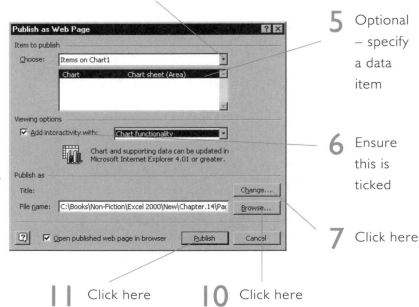

6 Ensure this is ticked

7 Click here

11 Click here   **10** Click here

Re step 10 – complete the Browse dialog which launches, in line with the procedures described in 'Publishing workbooks non-interactively' on page 63. Finally, perform step 11.

8 Name the published chart

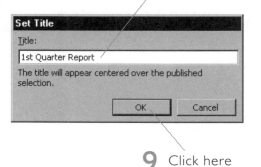

9 Click here

Inserting pictures

You can insert pictures into worksheets in two ways:

- with the Office Clip Gallery

- using a separate dialog

Inserting pictures via the Clip Gallery

First, position the insertion point at the location within the active worksheet where you want to insert the picture. Pull down the Insert menu and click Picture, Clip Art. Do the following:

All clips have associated keywords. You can use these to locate clips. Click in this field in the Gallery:

Type one or more words. . .

Now type in one or more keywords. Finally, press Enter – any relevant clips display.

| Ensure the Pictures tab is activated

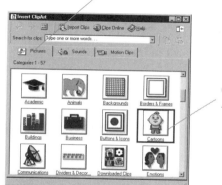

2 Click a category

Re step 2 – the Clip Gallery organises clips under overall categories.

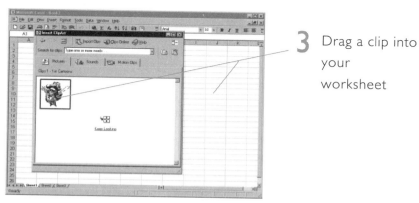

3 Drag a clip into your worksheet

To see more Gallery clips, carry out the following procedure. Click this:

Keep Looking

4 Release the mouse button – Excel 2000 inserts the picture

Once inserted into a worksheet, pictures can be resized and moved in the normal way.

Inserting pictures – the dialog route

First, position the insertion point at the location within the active worksheet where you want to insert the picture. Pull down the Insert menu and do the following:

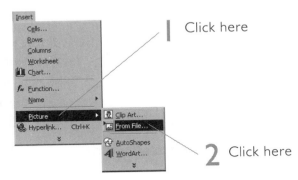

1 Click here

2 Click here

You can also insert pictures onto chart walls – see the HOT TIP on page 170.

4 Click here. In the drop-down list, click the drive/folder that hosts the picture

Excel 2000 provides a preview of what the picture will look like when it's been imported. (See the Preview box on the right of the dialog.)

6 Click here

If your system is currently displaying only 256 colours, pictures may not view correctly. To correct this, change to a higher display setting – see your Windows documentation for how to do this.

3 Make sure All Pictures... is shown. If it isn't, click the arrow and select it from the drop-down list

5 Click a picture file

Using AutoShapes

If you want to add text to an AutoShape, right-click it. In the menu, click Add Text. The insertion point appears inside the figure; type in the text. Click outside the AutoShape.

AutoShapes represent an extraordinarily flexible and easy-to-use way to insert a wide variety of shapes into your worksheets. Once inserted, they can be:

- resized

- rotated/flipped

You can also add text to AutoShapes – see the HOT TIPS. Excel 2000 automatically aligns text optimally.

Inserting an AutoShape

Refer to the Drawing toolbar – if it isn't currently visible, pull down the View menu and click Toolbars, Drawing. Do the following:

Changes you make to an AutoShape also affect any inserted text.

Re step 3 – for access to extra autoshapes, click More AutoShapes. In the Clip Gallery, locate the required shape then drag it into your worksheet.

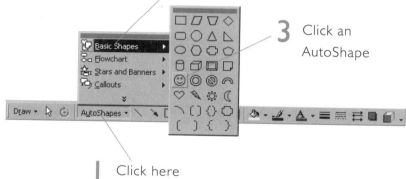

2 Click an AutoShape category

3 Click an AutoShape

Click here

Now carry out these steps:

Re step 6 – hold down Shift as you drag to maintain the original height/width relationship.

4. Place the mouse pointer where you want your AutoShape to start

5. Hold down the left mouse button

6. Drag out the shape

7. Release the mouse button when you've finished

Resizing AutoShapes

Select the AutoShape. Now do the following:

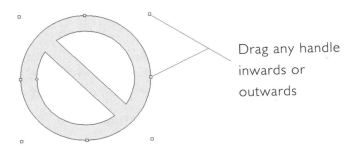

Drag any handle
inwards or
outwards

Rotating AutoShapes

Select the AutoShape. Now refer to the Drawing toolbar and
do the following:

To rotate in
90° stages,
don't follow
steps 1 or 2.
Instead, do the
following. Click here:
In the menu, click Rotate
or Flip. In the sub-menu,
click Rotate Left or Rotate
Right.

Click here

2 Position the mouse pointer over one of the
handles – it changes to a rotation symbol

To 'flip' an
AutoShape,
select it. Click
the Draw
button in the
Drawing toolbar. In the
menu, click Rotate or Flip,
followed by Flip Horizontal
or Flip Vertical.

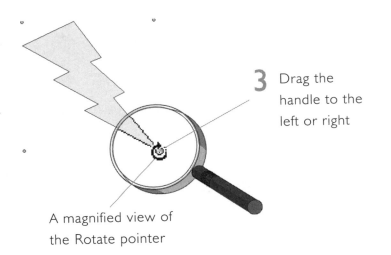

3 Drag the
handle to the
left or right

A magnified view of
the Rotate pointer

Using macros

This chapter shows you how to automate frequently performed tasks by recording them as macros and playing them back whenever necessary. You'll also learn to associate the macros you create with toolbar buttons, keystrokes and menu entries, to make it even easier and more convenient to use macros.

Covers

Chapter Fifteen

Recording a macro

Excel 2000 lets you automate any task which you undertake frequently. You do this by recording it as a macro. A macro is a recorded series of commands which can be 'rerun' at will. Using macros can save you a considerable amount of time and effort.

Once recorded, macros can be rerun:

- with the use of a special dialog

- by clicking a toolbar button

- by pressing a keystroke combination (defined when you record the macro)

- by clicking a special menu entry

Here, we're recording a macro which will embolden and italicise cell contents in one operation (actions which can already be implemented separately by pressing Ctrl+B and Ctrl+I respectively).

This is a very simple example, for the sake of clarity; however, you can easily record complex procedures as macros.

Recording a macro

First, plan out (preferably on paper) the precise sequence of actions involved in the task you want to record. Pull down the Tools menu and do the following:

1 Click here

2 Click here

...cont'd

Re step 4 – Excel 2000 assumes you want the shortcut key which will launch the macro to be:

Ctrl+?

where ? is any letter.
However, you can also incorporate Shift into any keystroke combination; simply hold down one Shift key as you type in the letter. For example, to have the macro invoked by pressing:

Ctrl+Shift+H

hold down Shift and type in 'h' (omit the quotes).

Now carry out the following steps:

3 Name the macro

5 Optional – type in extra descriptive text

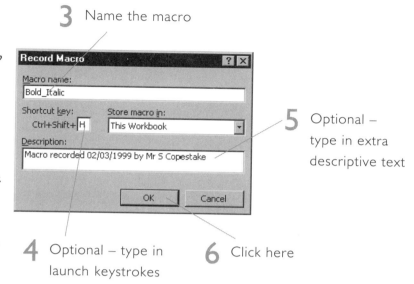

4 Optional – type in launch keystrokes

6 Click here

Perform the actions you want to record. When you've finished, do the following:

The Stop Recording toolbar

7 Click here

Running a macro

You can run macros in a variety of ways.

The dialog route

First, select the cells you want to apply the macro to. Pull down the Tools menu and carry out the following steps:

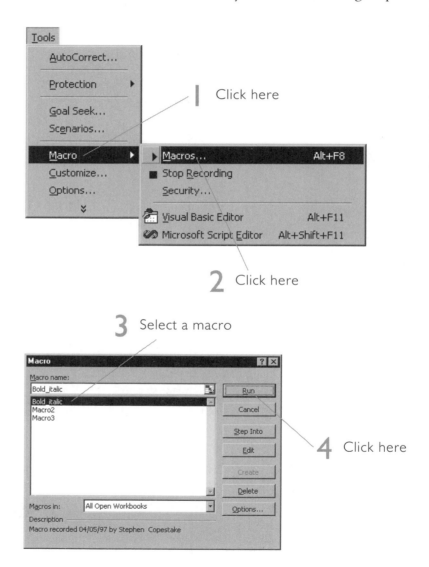

1 Click here

2 Click here

3 Select a macro

4 Click here

See the HOT TIP on page 186 for how to impose macros as entries on menus.

The menu route

First, select the cells you want to apply the macro to. Pull down the menu to which you've added the macro and do the following:

Here, the macro entry has been added to the Format menu.

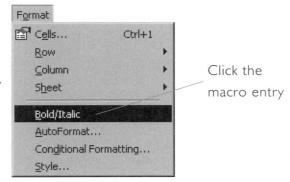

Click the macro entry

The toolbar route

In the example on the immediate right, the macro button has been added to the Formatting toolbar (expanded to display more than the default number of buttons).

If you've created a special toolbar button and allocated the macro to it (see page 186 for how to do this), select the relevant cell(s) and do the following:

Click here

The keystroke route

By default, macro toolbar buttons look like this:

If you've allocated a keystroke combination to the macro during the creation process (see page 183 for how to do this), select the cell(s) you want to amend and press the relevant keys.

For instance (and to continue the original example from pages 182-183), to italicise and embolden cell contents in one operation, press Ctrl+Shift+H.

Assigning macros to toolbars

To assign a macro as a new button on a toolbar, first make sure the toolbar is visible (see page 11 for how to do this). Move the mouse pointer over the toolbar and right-click once. In the menu which appears, click Customize. Now do the following:

You can add macros as menu entries. Follow steps 1 & 2. In step 3, drag this button:

Custom Menu Item

onto the menu of your choice. Now right-click the resultant menu entry. In the menu which launches, carry out steps 6-7. Perform step 8 to allocate a macro to the menu entry.

Finally, carry out step 9.

1 Ensure this tab is active

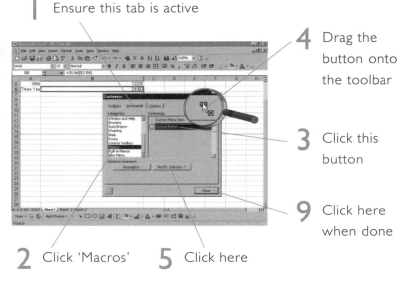

4 Drag the button onto the toolbar

3 Click this button

9 Click here when done

2 Click 'Macros' 5 Click here

Re step 6 – ensure you leave in the ampersand – for instance, you could type in:

&Bold/Italic

6 Name the button

7 Click here

8 Double-click the macro you want to assign to the new button

Index

n

Number formats, changing   40

o

Office Assistant   25–28
  Asking questions of   28
  Closing windows   26
  Hiding   26
  Launching   26
  Save prompt   171–172
  Sending queries to the Web from   28
  Viewing tips   27
Outlining
  Applying   137
  Defined   137
  Hiding outlined data   138
  Removing   139
  The Outline Level Bar   137

p

Page Break Preview   160, 166
Page breaks
  Automatic, viewing   163
  Manual, inserting   163
Page numbering. *See* Page setup, Page numbering
Page setup
  An overview   160
  Header/footer options   164
  Margin options   163
  Page numbering   166
  Page options   162

Worksheet options   161
Patterns
  Applying   148
Pictures
  Inserting
    Into charts   170
    Into worksheets   177, 178
    Previewing before insertion   178
PivotCharts
  Creating from PivotTables   122
PivotTables
  AutoFormats
    Applying to   122
  Creating   121
Precedents
  In recalculation   112
Print areas   161
Print Preview   61
  Launching   165
  Toolbar   166
  Using   166

q

Quick File Switching   29

r

R1C1 referencing   76
Range Finder   43
Range operator   84
Ranges   19–20
Redoing actions   34
Reference operators   84
References
  Absolute   75
  Relative   74
'Round-tripping'   69. *See also* HTML file format
    and Workbooks, Saving to HTML